"At a point when education, health and social care are in complete turmoil and individuals are struggling to access the support, services and provision that they require, this publication will offer a welcome discourse to help parents and professionals to better understand the political and social landscape that we are currently living and working in."

Lorraine Petersen, *OBE – Educational Consultant*

"Dr Rona Tutt and Paul Williams are perfectly placed to navigate through this challenging time of changing policy. With real world examples of great practice, they showcase innovative approaches to achieving an integrated system to support children and young people and their families effectively and responsively. This book offers an important tool in achieving meaningful and lasting change."

Dr Amelia Roberts, *Associate Professor and Deputy Director of UCL Centre for Inclusive Education, Associate Professor (Teaching) and Vice Dean (Enterprise)*

"This book is designed for the busy educational professional. Navigating through the current complexities of education legislation can be time consuming. Written with clarity and insight this is the ideal reference text to guide teachers and other professionals to meaningful, child centred solutions."

Professor Barry Carpenter, *CBE, D.Litt., Professor of Mental Health in Education, Oxford Brookes University*

A Guide to Best Practice in Special Education, Health and Social Care

A Guide to Best Practice in Special Education, Health and Social Care explores and explains the changes in governmental policies across the education, health and social care services, and what they mean for young individuals, parents and professionals.

In a period of significant change, many practitioners need to understand the government's plans for bringing about a more efficient, effective and sustainable system to meet the needs of young people and their families. Without trawling through reviews, green papers, white papers and bills, this book not only explains the significance of recent events, but provides practical examples, in the form of conversations and case studies, about how parents and professionals are making change happen. With decades of experience, Rona Tutt and Paul Williams delve deep into the separate origins of the three strands – the SEND review, the review of children's social care, and the Health and Care Act 2022. The book explores how pupils in different types of schools can have their needs met more effectively; how to make better use of available resources; and how to create a culture of mutual respect across all the three services.

A Guide to Best Practice in Special Education, Health and Social Care not only fills in gaps in readers' knowledge about the working of all three services, but provides innovative examples of how change is happening at ground level. People of all age groups working in schools and seeking to enhance their knowledge will find it to be an essential read. It will also be of interest to parents and professionals from across health and social care.

Rona Tutt has an OBE for her services to special needs education. She is a former head teacher, Past President of the National Association of Head Teachers (NAHT) and a fellow of UCL's Centre for Inclusive Education (CIE).

Paul Williams has been the head teacher of two special schools in London. He was on NAHT's National Executive for many years and chair of the SEND Council. He has also been a national leader of education (NLE).

A Guide to Best Practice in Special Education, Health and Social Care

Making the System Work to Meet the Needs of Children, Young People and Their Families

Rona Tutt and Paul Williams

Routledge
Taylor & Francis Group
LONDON AND NEW YORK

Designed cover image: © Getty Images

First published 2023
by Routledge
4 Park Square, Milton Park, Abingdon, Oxon OX14 4RN

and by Routledge
605 Third Avenue, New York, NY 10158

Routledge is an imprint of the Taylor & Francis Group, an informa business

© 2023 Rona Tutt and Paul Williams

British Library Cataloguing-in-Publication Data
A catalogue record for this book is available from the British Library

Library of Congress Cataloging-in-Publication Data
Names: Tutt, Rona, author. | Williams, Paul, 1950- author.
Title: A guide to best practice in special education, health and social
care : making the system work to meet the needs of children, young
people and their families / Rona Tutt and Paul Williams.
Description: First edition. | New York : Routledge, 2023. | Includes
bibliographical references and index.
Identifiers: LCCN 2022055410 (print) | LCCN 2022055411 (ebook) | ISBN
9781032366760 (hbk) | ISBN 9781032366753 (pbk) | ISBN 9781003333203 (ebk)
Subjects: LCSH: Special education--Great Britain. | Inclusive
education--Great Britain. | Children with disabilities--Education--Great
Britain. | Special education--Government policy--Great Britain. |
Special education--Law and legislation--Great Britain. | Inclusive
education--Government policy--Great Britain. | Children with
disabilities--Education--Government policy--Great Britain. | Children
with disabilities--Education--Law and legislation--Great Britain. |
Special education teachers--Great Britain--In-service training.
Classification: LCC LC3986.G7 T869 2023 (print) | LCC LC3986.G7 (ebook) |
DDC 371.90941--dc23/eng/20230201
LC record available at https://lccn.loc.gov/2022055410
LC ebook record available at https://lccn.loc.gov/2022055411

ISBN: 978-1-032-36676-0 (hbk)
ISBN: 978-1-032-36675-3 (pbk)
ISBN: 978-1-003-33320-3 (ebk)

DOI: 10.4324/9781003333203

Typeset in Bembo
by SPi Technologies India Pvt Ltd (Straive)

We would like to dedicate this book to all those who have led the way in communicating across professional boundaries, in order to meet the needs of children, young people, and their families.

Contents

Acknowledgements

Richard Broadhurst   Social Worker and Assistant Head Teacher Baycroft School, Fareham, Hampshire

Jane Carter   Head of Integrated Disability Services, Warwickshire CC

David Duncan   Former Head Teacher and current SEMH specialist

Timothy Ellis   Strategic Lead, Leamington LAMP, Leamington Spa, Warwickshire

Alan Garnett   Head Teacher North Primary School and Nursery, Colchester, Essex

Julia James   Principal Bedelsford School and SW Regional Lead for Orchard Hill College and Academy Trust

Carol Kelsey   National Network of Parent Carer Forums, Eastern Region National Representative

Elaine McWilliams   SENCO, The Valley School, Stevenage, Hertfordshire

Christopher Miller   Chair of Harrow's Safeguarding Board and Scrutineer of Harrow's Safeguarding Children's Partnership

Tracy Noble   Team Manager for Hertfordshire's Learning Difficulties and Disabilities Team of Services for Young People

Patrick O'Dwyer   Director of Education, Harrow

David Pearce   Head Teacher, The Valley School, Stevenage, Hertfordshire

Simon Reakes   Head of Publishing, Ruskin Mill Trust, Nailsworth, Gloucestershire

Lesley Reeves Costi   Co-Head, Heathlands School, St Albans, Hertfordshire

Diana Robinson   SEN Expert on Independent Review Panels for Exclusions

Ian Taylor   NAHT Regional Organiser for East Midlands and Yorkshire

Nick Whittaker   Founder of the charity Climbing for All, Sheffield, former HMI and specialist adviser for SEND at Ofsted

Abbreviations

AAC	Augmentative and Alternative Communication
ADHD	Attention Deficit Hyperactivity Disorder
AET	Autism Education Trust
AHDC	Aiming High for Disabled Children
ALN	Additional Learning Needs
AP	Alternative Provision
ASD	Autistic Spectrum Disorder
BASW	British Association of Social Workers
BATOD	British Association of Teachers of the Deaf
BESD	Behaviour, Emotional and Social Development
BIS	Department for Business, Innovation and Skills
BSL	British Sign Language
BTEC	Business and Technology Education Council
CAMHS	Child and Adolescent Mental Health Services
CCG	Clinical Commissioning Group
CDC	Council for Disabled Children
CEC	Careers Enterprise Company
CEO	Chief Education Officer
CfAS	Climbing for All Sheffield
CiC	Children in Care
CiN	Children in Need
CLDD	Complex Learning Difficulties and Disabilities
CODA	Children of Deaf Adults
CoP	Code of Practice
CPD	Continuing Professional Development
CQC	Care Quality Commission
CTC	City Technology College
CYP	Children and Young People
DBV	Delivering Better Value
DCO	Designated Clinical Officer
DLD	Developmental Language Disorder
DCS	Director of Children's Services
DCSF	Department for Children, Schools and Families
DDA	Disability Discrimination Act

DfE	Department for Education
DHSC	Department of Health and Social Care
DLD	Developmental Language Disorder
DLUHC	Department for Levelling Up, Housing and Communities
DMO	Designated Medical Officer
DoH	Department of Health
DSG	Dedicated Schools Grant
DSL	Designated Safeguarding Lead
EAL	English as an Additional Language
EAZ	Education Action Zone
EBacc	English Baccalaureate
EBD	Emotional and Behavioural Difficulties
ECF	Early Career Framework
ECM	Every Child Matters
EHCP	Education, Health and Care Plan
EIA	Education Investment Area
EMAS	Ethnic Minority Achievement Service
EMHP	Education Mental Health Practitioner
EOB	Enemy of Boredom
EP	Educational Psychologist
EPI	Education Policy Institute
EPS	Educational Psychology Service
ESFA	Education and Skills Funding Agency
EWO	Education Welfare Officer
FASD	Foetal Alcohol Spectrum Disorder
FE	Further Education
FGC	Family Group Conference
FLT	Flexible Learning Team
FSM	Free School Meals
GCSE	General Certificate of Secondary Education
GDD	Global Developmental Delay
GDP	Governors Disciplinary Panel
GLA	Greater London Authority
GLC	Greater London Council
GP	General Practitioner
GSP	Green Social Prescribing
HAF	Holiday Activities and Food Programme
HE	Higher Education
HEE	Health Education England
HEI	Higher Education Institute
HI	Hearing Impairment
HLE	Healthy Life Expectancy
HMCI	Her Majesty's Chief Inspector (up to 08.09.22)
HMCI	His Majesty's Chief Inspector (from 08.09.22)
HMI	Her Majesty's Inspector
HNF	High Needs Funding

HPIG	Health Policy Influencing Group
HTQ	Higher Technical Qualification
HWB	Health and Wellbeing Board
ICB	Integrated Care Board
ICP	Integrated Care Partnership
ICS	Integrated Care System
ICT	Information and Communications Technology
IDS	Integrated Disabilities Service
IfAT	Institute for Apprenticeships and Technical Education
IFS	Institute of Fiscal Studies
ILACS	Inspecting Local Authority Children's Services
INSET	In-Service Training
IoT	Institutes of Technology
IRP	Independent Review Panel
ISI	Independent Schools Inspectorate
JSNA	Joint Strategic Needs Assessment
KCSiE	Keeping Children Safe in Education
LA	Local Authority
LAAO	Local Authority Attendance Officer
LAC	Looked After Child
LADO	Local Authority Designated Officer
LD	Learning Difficulties
LDA	Learning Difficulties Assessment
LDD	Learning Difficulties and Disabilities
LEA	Local Education Authority
LEP	Local Enterprise Partnership
LFF	Local Funding Formula
LGA	Local Government Association
LMS	Local Management of Schools
LSB	Local Safeguarding Board
LSIP	Life Skills Improvement Plan
MAT	Multi Academy Trust
MHST	Mental Health Support Team
MLD	Moderate Learning Difficulties
MSI	Multi-Sensory Impairment
NAHT	National Association of Head Teachers
NAO	National Audit Office
NAS	National Autistic Society
NatSIP	National Association for Sensory Impairment Partnershi
NASENCO	National Award for SEN Coordination
NAVSH	National Association of Virtual School Heads
NCB	National Children's Bureau
NCSL	National College for School Leadership
NEET	Not in Education, Employment or Training
NFF	National Funding Formula
NHS	National Health Service

NHSC	National Health Service Confederation
NHSE	National Health Service England
NHSI	NHS Improvement
NNATPIP	National Network of Advisory Teachers for Physically Impaired Pupils
NNPCF	National Network of Parent Carer Forums
NPF	National Professional Framework
NPQ	National Professional Qualification
NTP	National Tutoring Programme
OA	Opportunity Area
Ofsted	Office for Standards in Education
OHID	Office for Health Improvement and Disparities
OT	Occupational Therapist
PA	Personal Assistant
PCF	Professional Capabilities Framework
PCT	Primary Care Trust
PD	Physical Disabilities
PDA	Pathalogical Demand Avoidance
pdnet	Network for Those Supporting Learners with a Physical Disability
PE	Physical Education
PGCE	Post Graduate Certificate in Education
PHE	Public Health England
PMLD	Profound and Multiple Learning Difficulties
PNI	Physical and Neurological Impairment
PODD	Pragmatic, Organised, Dynamic Display
PRU	Pupil Referral Unit
PSHE	Personal. Social and Health Education/ Personal, Social, Health and Economic Education
PSO	Police Support Officer
PSTE	Practical Skills Therapeutic Education
PVI	Private, Voluntary and Independent
QAA	Quality Assurance Agency
QCA	Qualifications and Curriculum Authority
RD	Regional Director
RoAPT	Register of Apprenticeship Training
RRSA	Rights Respecting Schools Award
RSC	Regional Schools Commissioner
RSE	Relationships and Sex Education
RSHE	Relationships, Sex and Health Education
SaLT	Speech and Language Therapy
SCR	Single Central Record
SEF	Self Evaluation Form
SEMH	Social, Emotional and Mental Health Difficulties
SENCO	Special Education Needs Coordinator
SEND	Special Educational Needs and Disability
SENDA	Special Educational Needs and Disability Act

SENDIASS	SEND Information, Advice and Support Services
SENDIST	Special Educational Needs and Disability Tribunal
SFA	SEND Financial Adviser
SHA	Strategic Health Authority
SLCN	Speech, Language and Communication Needs
SLD	Severe Learning Difficulties
SLT	Senior Leadership Team
SMHL	Senior Mental Health Lead
SpLD	Specific Learning Difficulties
SPP	Service Pupil Premium
SSE	Sign Supported English
STEM	Science, Technology, Engineering and Maths
STP	Sustainability and Transformation Plan
STS	Specialist Teaching Service
SWiS	Social Workers in Schools
TA	Teaching Assistant
TAC	Team Around the Child
ToD	Teacher of the Deaf
UNCRC	United Nations Convention on the Rights of the Child
USP	Unique Selling Point
UTC	University Technical Colleges
VI	Visual Impairment
VSH	Virtual School Headteacher
WSoA	Written Statement of Action
YoT	Youth Offending Team

Introductory chapter
Why this book has been written

> Services need to be shaped by and responsive to children, young people and families, not designed around professional boundaries.
>
> (The Children's Plan 2007: 06)

This book is divided into two parts. Part One, "Accommodating All Young People", has four chapters which explain in some detail how the education, health and social care services have developed and how they have reached simultaneously a significant moment in time. Part Two has a further four chapters and there is a greater emphasis on how the changes are making a difference to the lives of the professionals involved, as well as to children, young people, and their families. Comments, conversations, and case studies are woven through the book. The final chapter brings together some of the themes running throughout and points the way forward for a more co-ordinated system, which would enhance the wellbeing and effectiveness of professionals working across the services as well as improving the experiences of those who rely on them.

The first part of this introductory chapter sets out some of the structures that exist at local, regional, and national level in terms of how the services of education, health, and social care are delivered to young people and their families. The second part of the chapter explains why this is the right time to make another push for interagency working. There is a conversation with a director of education and the chapter ends with the views of Ian Taylor, who has been both a head teacher and worked in local authorities (LAs) before embarking on another role in education.

Ever since the Every Child Matters (ECM) agenda, which was launched in 2003 following Lord Laming's inquiry into the tragic death of eight-year-old Victoria Climbie, there has been a recognition that the way to protect children and give them the chance of a safe, happy, and fulfilled childhood is for the three services of education, health, and social care to work more closely together, along with other partners and, of course, with parents and the young people themselves. Changes have been made at national, local, and individual level, to try to bring about a more joined-up and person-centred way of working, but the goal has remained partly out of reach. This has not been helped by the constant churn of change. Whether it is the relentless reforms to education; the constant reconfiguring of the health service; or the failure to learn lessons every time there is some

DOI: 10.4324/9781003333203-1

catastrophe in children's social care, interagency working still has a long way to go. Sometimes, children seem to disappear from the system and that is worrying enough. In other cases, such as Victoria's, they are known to many people and services, but due to a lack of sharing information, building up a more complete picture does not happen. To play even a very small part in moving this agenda forward is the reason why this book has been written.

The importance of the ECM Green Paper

The ECM Green Paper contained four main proposals based on:

- Supporting Parents and Carers
- Early Intervention and Effective Protection
- Accountability and Integration – Locally, Regionally, Nationally
- Workforce Reform

These four proposals highlighted what needed to be done 20 years ago and all four might still be said to be a work in progress. The first of these, for example, was the need to support families, and steps have been taken to see parents as equal partners rather than being told by professionals what they should do. This is exemplified in education, health, and care plans (EHCPs), which replaced "statements" for children with more complex needs as part of the SEND reforms of 2014. The change of name from statement to EHCP is significant. Not only are the views of children and their parents seen as an important part of the process, but all three services are meant to be involved. In the event, these plans have been of variable quality and time consuming to produce.

As well as the main proposals, the ECM Green Paper included five outcomes. These had arisen from what children had said mattered to them the most:

- Being healthy
- Staying safe
- Enjoying and achieving
- Making a positive contribution
- Economic wellbeing.

These have been echoed in part since then by the National Health Service (NHS) Five Steps to Mental Wellbeing:

1. Connect with other people
2. Be physically active
3. Learn new skills
4. Give to others
5. Pay attention to the present moment (mindfulness).

The year after the ECM Green Paper appeared, the Children Act 2004 was passed in order to implement the proposals. In his foreword, Prime Minister Tony Blair wrote about the importance of, *"requiring local authorities to bring together in one place under one person services for children"*. Combining the role of director of education with the director of children's social care at local authority (LA) level was a significant step forward in terms of interagency working. As some readers may not be familiar with the workings of government at local and national level, the next part of this chapter has been written to provide a basis for what is covered in the rest of the book.

Local levels of government

The significant change at local level already referred to was the requirement for larger local authorities, known as "upper tier" LAs, to appoint a director of children's services (DCS) covering both education and children's social services, which had previously been under two separate directors. Although it only covered education and social care, a duty was placed on all LAs to cooperate with other LAs, agencies, and bodies to improve the wellbeing of children. In addition to the DCS, a lead member for children's services is also a requirement. They are appointed from those who have been elected as county councillors.

LA structures

There are 152 LAs in England. They are divided into two-tier authorities and unitary authorities. The other nations of the UK have unitary authorities only.

Information point: Local authority structures

Local authorities in England are divided into:

1. Two tier authorities where local government is divided between:
       24 county councils (upper tier)
       181 district councils (lower tier)
2. Unitary authorities where there is a single tier of government. These include:
       58 unitaries
       36 metropolitan districts (called either district councils, borough councils or city councils)
       32 London boroughs*
         – City of London
         – Scilly Isles

★ Although the Greater London Council (GLC) was dissolved in 1986, in 2000 the Greater London Authority (GLA) was established to enable sharing across London boroughs.

Models of local government have to be operated in one of the following ways:

- A mayor and cabinet executive
- A leader and cabinet executive
- The committee system
- Other arrangements approved by the secretary of state

Combined authorities

In addition, there are combined authorities where two or more LAs decide to work together. This does not replace the existing LAs, but allows them to work together and make collective decisions. At the time of writing, there are ten combined authorities:

- Cambridgeshire and Peterborough
- Greater Manchester
- Liverpool City Region
- North East
- North of Tyne
- South Yorkshire
- Tees Valley
- West Midlands
- West of England
- West Yorkshire.

Different types of schools

For those unfamiliar with the range of schools that have developed over time in England, it may be a confusing picture; not only because of the diversity, but also because of the way they are described. For example, public schools are the most exclusive type of independent or private schools, accessible mainly to those who can afford the substantial fees. Academies are described as independent state funded schools because they are outside the control of the LA, yet, unlike independent schools, are funded directly by government. Schools in England include:

Community schools, also known as maintained schools, which may be

- Voluntary-aided schools (often faith schools)
- Foundation schools (formerly grant-maintained)
- Voluntary-controlled schools (often faith schools)
- Grammar schools (allowed to select pupils on ability)

Special schools are often community schools, but may be academies, non-maintained, or independent schools.

Alternative provision schools may be run by the LA or other providers.

Academies may be:

- Standalone academies
- Multi Academy Trusts (MATs)
- Free Schools
- University Technical Colleges (UTCs)
- City Technology Colleges (CTCs)

Independent schools are also known as private or public schools.

Some of the chapters in this book have conversations and case studies about the different types of schools, as well as insights from those who have experience of working in LAs. The first of these conversations was held before the Schools Bill was withdrawn.

In conversation with Patrick O'Dwyer, Director of Education, Harrow

Q. How far does your work in education overlap with children's social care?

A. The vast majority of children are not involved with social care, but we have some significant areas where we do link, such as where children are out of school, who, in some cases need early support (non-statutory) assistance, and some of whom are known to statutory social care services. Children who are known to social care but attend school regularly require less engagement from education services unless they are looked after by the LA or have a special educational need. Some children and young people with SEND are supported by the care team for children with disabilities, who play an integral part in decision-making regarding the child or young person's education, particularly where a residential placement may be required. Social care is engaged in the development of all EHC plans through carrying out an assessment of need and making the appropriate commentary and any required provision.

Q. What is your relationship with health services as regards children's physical and mental health?

A. Relationships are good. There are challenges which will be familiar to all LAs and health services. Some of this relates to recent rises in demand for specialist services, particularly mental health and therapy services. For children and young people, we hold joint discussions about what should be charged to health or to education. Health and education can differ on the allocation of funds on occasion. However, education will always make the decision that is right for the child in consultation with parents.

Q. As the government gives a sum of money to LAs to cover both education and children's social care, how does the proportion for each service get decided?

A. Funding for schools and other education provision comes from the Dedicated Schools Grant (DSG) and is allocated to the LA via national funding formulae for the four blocks of the DSG. The funding in the schools block is then allocated to mainstream schools using the local funding formula (LFF). In Harrow, the NFF has been adopted as the LFF. The Schools Forum is consulted on the LFF but the LA ultimately decides the formula. High needs block commissioning is a matter for the LA in consultation with schools and the schools forum. The LA is funded from a number of sources including council tax, government grants, and subsidies. Funding is allocated according to local demand and priorities and based on spending levels required to deliver statutory services.

Q. What do you think of the drive towards academisation in the Schools Bill?

A. Our view is that this is a matter for school governing bodies. The LA will listen to its schools and will consider setting up an LA–established MAT if that is the wish of maintained schools. It is clear that the LA will not be "running" these MATS. The legislation on academies is not being changed in that sense. As far as SEND is concerned the type of school is not a significant factor overall in Harrow. The duties on the LA and the school are the same.

Q. If the Bill goes through without much alteration, what impact, both positive and negative, do you think it might have on your role?

A. As for the White Paper, the main impact has already happened with the previous removal of the School Monitoring Grant by the DFE against the wishes of the vast majority in consultation. This makes it extremely difficult for LAs to carry on a close relationship with their schools and others in relation to improvement in the broadest sense. For us that includes developing a sector-led school-to-school system of improvement in which the LA is a partner. We can seek funding from the Schools Forum but that is not guaranteed. Duties on the LA have not been removed. This will have an effect on partnership building and school improvement and that relationship is key to building general trust on which all services rely to some degree. The White Paper will strengthen our role in school attendance but there appears to be no funding to cover this expanded expectation. There are parts of the White Paper on professional development which are very welcome. Much of the White Paper reflects an existing direction of movement.

Q. What do you think of the SEND Green Paper? Will it bring about better outcomes for CYP with SEND? Is there funding to support the changes?

A. The Green Paper is, for the most part, an iteration of what was learned as best practice from the first round of Area SEN inspections. In this sense, there are no major surprises in it. We were inspected in 2019, and it was encouraging to have it confirmed that we were on the right track in embedding the 2014 SEND Reforms. We see the Green Paper as an encouragement to embed that good practice for the future, and, in particular, the importance of joint working and co-production.

Q. Have there been cutbacks in the authority to SEND support teams and specialist teachers?

A. No, but it is challenging to expand in order to cover a growing demand and there are specific challenges in recruiting educational psychologists (EPs) and therapists. The funding here primarily comes from the high needs block. The intention is for all the needs for support identified in an EHCP to be met. Harrow is not alone in actively seeking to manage its high need funding.

Q. How have you managed any growing demand for EHC needs assessments or special school places?

A. In recent years, we have provided additional funding for our SEN Assessment and Review Service and for the Educational Psychology Service in order to meet demand. We have also increased the number of additional resourced mainstream schools in the borough and changed the intake of some local special schools to ensure that more places are found to meet demand in borough. This is part of a "system shift" that is taking place.

Q. What are your thoughts on the recommendations of the independent review of children's social care about schools becoming part of Safeguarding Boards?

A. School representatives sit on our safeguarding children's board already and play a key role at all levels. Whilst this should be supported, we need to be realistic about school capacity, which is already very stretched.

Patrick has touched on a number of topics which are picked up later in this book. This includes the government's drive for academisation, funding issues, safeguarding, and the struggle to support young learners when not only money, but EPs, therapists, and specialist teachers are in short supply. Also, he gives an insight into the way a unitary authority manages to ensure that working across the services is given a high priority.

National and regional levels of government

In 2018, at government level, health and social care were amalgamated in England when the Department of Health and Social Care (DHSC) was formed, leaving education as the one service outside this arrangement. Yet, at local level, as has been explained, combining education and children's social services departments had resulted in health being the odd one out.

More recently, at national level, and as part of the Levelling Up agenda (which is discussed in the next chapter), the government has had a Places for Growth programme, which sees government departments moving some of their work to cities across the UK by 2030. These moves are already underway.

The DfE, for instance, has established a Regions Group. This has led to increasing the number of Regional Schools Commissioners (RSCs) from eight to nine, so they match the DfE's nine regions. RSCs were established to oversee the work of the growing number of schools becoming academies in their area and to encourage other schools to join them.

Information point: DfE's Regions Group

The government's nine regional offices are in the geographical areas of:

London	North East	North West
Yorkshire and Humber	East Midlands	West Midlands
South East	East of England	South West

In February 2022, the Regional Schools Commissioners (RSCs) were expanded to nine.

In June 2022, the DfE announced that the RSCs would, in future, be known as regional directors, so they could lead the work of the regions. John Edwards was appointed as Director General of the Regions Group.

Since Summer 2022, the new Regions Group has been operational, working closely with the Education and Skills Funding Agency (ESFA) to consolidate post-16 policy and provide integrated delivery for schools and LAs, including children's social care and SEND.

In addition to the responsibilities already mentioned, the regional directors (RDs) will be:

- Addressing underperformance in academies and other schools as well as children's social care services
- Taking decisions on the creation, consolidation and growth of multi-academy trusts (MATs), and deciding on new free schools
- Supporting LAs to ensure that every local area has sufficient places for pupils
- Intervening in schools, academies, and children's social care services in LAs following SEND inspections and generating solutions to deliver rapid improvement
- Taking the lead on safeguarding cases in their region
- Delivering across a number of key programmes emerging from the schools' White Paper, the SEND Green Paper, and from the care review.

The three items mentioned in the final bullet point are central to the themes explored in this book as they cover health and social care, as well as education.

Children's Commissioners

Returning to the 2004 Children Act, another strand was the importance of listening to the voices of children and young people and to promote their interests. To this end, the post of Children's Commissioner was introduced. This brought England in line with the other countries of the UK. Wales appointed their first children's commissioner in 2001, Northern Ireland in 2003, and Scotland in 2004. Moving on a decade to 2014 and the Children and Families Act (which is mostly remembered for the previous set of SEND Reforms), the remit of the Children's Commissioner was increased by including a special responsibility for the rights of:

- Children who are in care
- Children who are leaving care
- Children who are living away from home
- Children who are receiving social care services.

Before these additions, the commissioner's statutory remit included understanding what children and young people think about things that affect them and encouraging decision makers always to take their best interests into account.

How services operate at national and local level across the UK

To bring together the first part of this Introductory Chapter, the following table is a summary of how the different parts of the UK have moved towards bringing the services of education, health, and social care closer together. As in England, there are some differences between what happens at local and national level.

A summary of the different approaches across the UK

Nations	Government level	Regional and local level
England	Department for Education (DfE) remains separate.	152 Local Authorities (LAs) responsible for education and children's social care.
	Separate departments for health and social care were combined in 2018 to form Department of Health and Social Care (DHSC).	NHS responsible for health through 40+ regional Integrated Care Systems (ICSs).
N. Ireland	Department of Education (DoE)	The Education Authority (EA) has five regional offices and is responsible for education and youth services.
	Department of Health (DoH) also has responsibility for social care services.	At local level, there are five Health and Social Care Trusts.
Scotland	Education Scotland is an executive agency of the Scottish government.	Local Authorities (LAs) are responsible for education and social care.
	Legislation in 2016 brought health and social care into a single, integrated system.	31 health and social care partnerships are run jointly by the LA and NHS.
Wales	Department for Education and Skills (DfES)	Each of the 22 local councils has a Director of Education.
	Department of Health and Social Services (DHSS)	The councils are also responsible for providing social care and working with seven NHS local health boards.

Why the book is being written now

As mentioned at the start of this Introductory Chapter, there was a reason for writing this book at this moment in time. The opportunity was created by education, health, and social care bringing out significant developments within the space of three months and with some synergy between them. In March 2022, the White Paper turned rapidly into the Schools Bill. The next day, the long-awaited SEND Review appeared in the form of a Green Paper. The timing of these last two documents was deliberate and showed a close connection between the two, even down to having similar covers. In April 2022, the Health and Social Care Bill became an Act, confirming its move to bring health and social care together through Integrated Care Systems (ICSs). (These are discussed in detail in Chapter 4 of this book). Last to appear was Josh MacAlister's *The Independent review of children's social care*, which came out in May 2022. The Executive Summary begins by saying: "This moment is a once in a generation opportunity to reset children's social care."

It could be argued that the right time to bring out a book is not while there are so many unfinished threads in the air. However, while writing this book, the Health and Care Bill has become an Act; the Schools White Paper has become a Bill; the consultation on the SEND Green Paper has been completed and The independent review of children's social care has published its final report. This provides plenty of material to draw on. In addition, there may be a hiatus as Liz Truss, who took over from Boris Johnson as Prime Minister in September 2022, was replaced within a matter of weeks by Rishi Sunak. He appointed Gillian Keegan as secretary of state for education and Stephen Barclay as secretary of state at the DHSC, both with largely new teams of ministers to support them.

So, despite these uncertainties, it is still a real opportunity to flag up the need for improved interagency working and the benefits of many other forms of partnerships. There never will be a time when everything is neatly wound up and, furthermore, what has not been finalised can still be influenced. While so much that is relevant to improving the lives of young people and their families is being discussed and debated, this is a moment in time that should not be wasted.

To conclude this Introductory Chapter, here is a second conversation. Ian Taylor has been a primary head teacher. He has worked with a number of LAs and is currently helping school leaders in his role as a regional organiser for the National Association of Head Teachers (NAHT). He gives an overview of his own experiences and some of the conclusions he has reached.

In conversation with Ian Taylor, former primary head teacher

Q. Could you sum up your experience so far in education?

A. I was a school leader for over 20 years, which included being head teacher at the same school in Southampton for 15 years. I worked in Hampshire – an upper tier county council with a number of district and parish councils. I also worked within Southampton City Council, a unitary authority with a single tier of local government. Here, I found it easier to make your voice heard as a professional than in a larger county. Southampton also had the advantage of the health boundary being coterminous with the

LA. I've also worked as a School Improvement Partner (SIP) in another LA and I'm now working as NAHT's Regional Organiser for East Midlands and Yorkshire, so I've seen education from many angles.

Q. How do you think support for schools might be improved?

A. To make support for pupils and the school community more effective, schools need an attached school nurse, social worker, police support officer, and an education welfare officer as a minimum. But this kind of support, together with interagency working, has become diminished and defunded over the years. It works best when there is regular contact so that individual cases can be discussed and agencies can get to know pupils and families. I was lucky when I was running a school to have only two different EWOs, each one staying in post for several years. With them I was able to discuss every pupil whose attendance was problematic and the kind of approach that might work in each individual circumstance. Sometimes the school nurse was involved as well. In this way, poor attendance became less of an issue. Schools increasingly need more regular psychological support for pupils. It is accepted that a child can be sent home if they are suffering with their *physical* health; schools have no such leeway for a pupil suffering with their *mental* health and who may be in crisis – causing damage or injuring themselves or others.

SENCOs continue to have a particularly tough job. As they are given different amounts of time to carry out their role, this can lead to inequality of provision. The number of pupils identified as having SEND varies from school to school, not just because of variations in intakes, but because of the inconsistencies in the identification process. A child may appear on the register in one school because of the difference in ability and performance to that of the wider cohort, rather than because they meet the definitions laid down in the SEND Code of Practice. They might not be identified as having such a need in another school. SENCOs are the ones who sometimes have to make decisions about which pupils have SEND and are entitled to additional support. If they try to intervene early, which is the right approach to take, they can be told to give the child more time to develop and early intervention can't happen. It is especially difficult for children in pre-school settings to get external agency support. Decisions made, sometimes in isolation, by a SENCO can mean a child landing up with a "label" that is rarely removed. Good practice would be to have some form of moderation or peer review, so that SENCOs from different schools could decide between them what level of support a child might need, but this takes time and money. A number of authorities in Wales are building this into their approach to the new ALN system.

When it comes to EHC plans and their reviews, the initial assessment, the plan itself, and the reviews of the plan are the responsibility of the LA. Yet SENCOs often find they are the ones trying to round up input from health, social care, and other agencies. When the provision specified on the plan, such as the need for speech and language therapy (SaLT), isn't forthcoming or adequate, there are plenty of examples of schools paying for it themselves rather than letting the pupil go without the help they need.

There is often a lack of trust between LAs and schools because the conversations that would lead to a better understanding of the situation from both perspectives don't take place. When deciding on any placements, for example where there is a difference of opinion, someone from the LA should visit the school and discuss why it would or would not be right for a prospective pupil to go there. It should be negotiated, rather than done at a distance without the LA officer knowing the impact it would have on the child or the school. The result can be a head teacher being made to take a pupil, whether or not their school is the right place for them. It doesn't help that schools are run on the idea that they should always be full, so then there's sometimes no capacity to take in more pupils, or provide for their needs. When they're forced to do so, provision can be stretched or ineffective.

Q. Drawing on your experience what is your advice on changing systems?

A. As most of us are resistant to change and prefer practices we're familiar with, when change is needed it can be difficult to persuade others to implement it. An additional problem is that, over the last couple of decades, there has been a move to form filling, tick boxes, and online systems, which have reduced the face-to-face, personal approaches which are the most successful. Another difficulty in effecting change, especially around the Code of Practice (CoP), is people being afraid to stray from following what have become, over time, cumbersome procedures – locally implemented but not necessarily laid down by the CoP. Some head teachers are good at "rule breaking", because they do what's best for the child, rather than being hamstrung by bureaucracy; but shortcuts around SEND issues, even ones which make sense, are often deemed too risky to take.

Taking a straightforward approach can prevent systems spinning out of control and bureaucracy overwhelming everything else. There are really only three things to consider: Do we have a system? Is it working or is it flawed? Is it being operated in the right way? So, make sure the system you need is in place, refine it when the need arises, and train people how to use it. Systems can be helpful in preventing things from going wrong and having a procedure to follow when they do. Detailed plans to make systems better, either within a school or an LA, are sometimes required, but they should always be simple to describe: Where are we now? (Position) Where do we want to be in, eg a year/two years? (Vision) What do we need to do to get there? (Mission). Overcomplication, either foisted on school leaders by local/national governments, or self-imposed (we're often our own worst enemy!), is a major factor in the poor retention of school leaders.

Q. What has been your experience of interagency working?

A. It was always difficult to get any consistency when working with social care, because the service is massively underfunded, relying on agency staff to fill the gaps caused by the constant turnover of staff. The "team around the child" approach has been around for a long time, but although it sounds as if everyone is working together, it's actually, in practice, about how each individual professional connects with the child. Yes, there is a team around the child, but it doesn't necessarily involve actual teamwork. What is needed is for people to meet, either virtually or face-to-face in a room, and have conversations about what is needed, making sure the child is at the centre of those discussions. Otherwise, people continue to work in silos and hide behind emails. Getting people in the same "room" is more possible with everyone becoming used to remote meetings. As well as making sure information is shared and everyone is working together, it can help to keep people in the loop and feel less alone in sorting out the right provision.

Another reason why the kinds of conversations Ian describes are so important is to do with safeguarding, which is covered in Chapter 4 of this book. Quite rightly, there is an emphasis on the voice of the parent, but very occasionally, there are parents who play professionals off against each other, and if the professionals don't share what they know, they may miss what is actually going on. Professionals-only meetings can reveal pieces of the jigsaw which protect a child. This is what went wrong in the case of Victoria Climbie, which is where this chapter began.

References

DCSF (2007) *The Children's Plan*. Available from https://assets.publishing.service.gov.uk/government/uploads/system/uploads/attachment_data/file/325111/2007-childrens-plan.pdf

DfE (2022) *Policy Paper – Opportunity for All Strong Schools with Great Teachers for Your Child*. Available from https://www.gov.uk/government/publications/opportunity-for-all-strong-schools-with-great-teachers-for-your-child

Gov.UK (2003). *The Victoria Climbie Inquiry: report of an enquiry by Lord Laming*. Available from https://www.gov.uk/government/publications/the-victoria-climbie-inquiry-report-of-an-inquiry-by-lord-laming

Gov.UK (2013) *Directors of Children's Services: Roles and Responsibilities*. Available from https://www.gov.uk/government/publications/directors-of-childrens-services-roles-and-responsibilities

Gov.UK (2014) *Children and Families Act*. Available from https://www.legislation.gov.uk/ukpga/2014/6/contents/enacted

Gov.UK (2022a). *Health and Care Act*. Available from https://bills.parliament.uk/bills/3022.

Gov.UK (2022b) *Regional Schools Commissioners' Decision Making Framework*. Available from https://www.gov.uk/government/organisations/regional-department-for-education-dfe-directors

Gov.UK (2022c) *Schools Bill*. Available from https://bills.parliament.uk/bills/3156

Gov.UK (2022d). *SEND Review: Right Support, Right Place, Right Time*. Available from https://assets.publishing.service.gov.uk/government/uploads/system/uploads/attachment_data/file/1063620/SEND_review_right_support_right_place_right_time_accessible.pdf

HM Government (2004) *Children Act*. Available from https://assets.publishing.service.gov.uk/government/uploads/system/uploads/attachment_data/file/942455/Working_together_to_safeguard_children_Statutory_framework_legislation_relevant_to_safeguarding_and_promoting_the_welfare_of_children.pdf

HM Treasury (2003) *Every Child Matters*. Available from https://assets.publishing.service.gov.uk/government/uploads/system/uploads/attachment_data/file/272064/5860.pdf

McAllister, J. (2022) *Independent Review of Children's Social Care: Final Report.* Available from https://childrenssocialcare.independent-review.uk

National Audit Office (2017) *A Short Guide to Local Authorities.* Available from https://www.nao.org.uk/wp-content/uploads/2017/09/A-Short-Guide-to-Local-Authorities.pdf

NHS (2019a) *Five Steps to Mental Wellbeing.* Available from https://www.nhs.uk/mental-health/self-help/guides-tools-and-activities/five-steps-to-mental-wellbeing/

Part I

Accommodating all young people

1 Recent developments across education, health and social care

> The need for a tightly coordinated, well-led set of changes across education, health and social care, with the aim of securing the very best provision and outcomes for CYP with SEND, could not be clearer.
>
> (Amanda Spielman, HMCI, June 2021)

Before the next three chapters complete Part One of this book by covering the SEND (special educational needs and/or disabilities) Green Paper, The independent review of children's social care and the Health and Care Act 2022 respectively, this chapter provides some background to these events. This includes the government's "Levelling Up" agenda, and the Schools White Paper and the Schools Bill that followed it, as well as dipping into post-16 developments in the shape of the Skills for Jobs White Paper leading to the Skills and Post-16 Act 2022. Further information about this age group is provided by a conversation with Tracy Noble, who spent many years as a careers adviser before specialising in supporting young people with learning difficulties and disabilities (LDD) into work or independent living.

As mentioned in the Introductory Chapter, there are references in this book to Green Papers, White Papers, Bills, and Acts. For example, the SEND Green Paper, the Schools White Paper, the Schools Bill, and the Health and Care Act have already been mentioned. Before getting into the substance of the chapter, it may be helpful to provide a brief synopsis of how government policy is made.

Information point: Green and White Papers, Bills, and Acts

Green Papers These are consultation documents used by the government to stimulate debate. They are worth responding to, as the responses can influence which ideas are carried forward and help to shape future legislation.

White Papers These are a statement of government policy on a particular subject and generally lead to a Bill. However, there may still be opportunities for influencing the contents.

DOI: 10.4324/9781003333203-3

Bills A Bill sets out a proposal for a new law, or a change to a law that already exists. Bills can either start their journey in the House of Commons or in the House of Lords, but will always be discussed by both Houses. Amendments may be made to the Bill during this time.

Acts Once a Bill has been agreed by both Houses of Parliament, the sovereign gives consent and the Bill becomes an Act.

This chapter begins by examining the Levelling Up White Paper before the Schools White Paper, which came a month later. The reason for this is made clear in the introduction to the Schools White Paper, *Opportunity for all: strong schools with great teachers for your child.* Here, it describes four documents which sit alongside each other as part of the government's wider agenda. These documents are:

- The Skills for Jobs White Paper
- The Levelling Up White Paper
- The SEND Review
- The Independent Care Review.

Time has moved on apace since these four documents were mentioned together, but they all remain relevant and will be considered. At the time of writing:

- *Skills for Jobs: Lifelong Learning for Opportunity and Growth* has resulted in the **Skills and Post-16 Act 2022**
- *Levelling Up the UK* led to the **Levelling-Up and Regeneration Bill**, which is on its way through parliament
- The SEND Review has resulted in a green paper: *SEND Review: Right support, Right place, Right time*, which is discussed thoroughly in Chapter 2 of this book
- The interim and final reports of *The independent review of children's social care* have been published and are looked at in detail in Chapter 3.

The Levelling Up White Paper

In February 2022, a month before both the Schools White Paper and the SEND Green Paper appeared, the government published *Levelling Up the United Kingdom*, setting out its ideas for rebalancing the UK economy and addressing regional inequalities. This wide-ranging document runs to nearly 300 pages. In his foreword, Boris Johnson, the Prime Minister at the time, said that he wanted to break the link between geography and destiny, so that where a person is born no longer determines how they will get on in life. A second foreword, signed jointly by Michael Gove, who was put in charge of the Department for Levelling Up, Housing and Communities (DLUHC) and Andrew Haldane, head of the Levelling

Up Taskforce, picked up this theme when they wrote: "*While talent is distributed evenly across the UK, opportunity is not*".

Responding to its publication, the NHS Confederation, which is a membership organisation speaking for the healthcare system in England, Wales, and Northern Ireland, placed this comment on its website:

> The white paper recognises the need to focus on both economic and social decision-making and the intrinsic links between health, education and skills and the wider economy. . . an important framing document for integrated care system and NHS leaders across the country.

Levelling Up the UK is divided into four chapters and the headings give an indication of the amount of ground it covers:

Chapter 1   The UK's Geographical Disparities: Drivers and Potential Policy Approaches
Chapter 2   Systems Reforms
Chapter 3   The Policy Programme
Chapter 4   Next Steps

The missions

In the second chapter, there is a table of 12 levelling up missions. These are divided into four focus areas. The four missions relevant to this book are clustered together under the second of these areas, which is headed: "Spread opportunities and improve public services, especially in those places where they are weakest". In brief, the four missions under this heading are:

Education   By 2030, the number of primary school children achieving the expected standard in reading, writing, and maths will have significantly increased.
Skills   By 2030, the number of people successfully completing high-quality skills training will have significantly increased in every area of the UK.
Health   By 2030, the gap in Healthy Life Expectancy (HLE) between local areas where it is highest and lowest will have narrowed.
Wellbeing   By 2030, wellbeing will have improved in every area of the UK.

In the third chapter, there is an explanation about these four missions being put together, because improving people's health, education, skills, and employment prospects gives everyone the opportunity to live fulfilling, healthy, and productive lives. Of these four missions, the overarching mission is seen as the one on wellbeing, which says it "*captures the extent to which people across the UK lead happy and fulfilling lives – the very essence of levelling up*" (2022d: 217).

In going on to explain each of these four missions more fully, the one on education uses the phrase "*eliminating illiteracy and innumeracy*", which is rather stronger than reaching an expected standard. This theme is picked up again in this chapter when discussing the Schools White Paper and, later on in Chapter 6 of this book. Another way in which the government plans to raise standards is by increasing the number of academies and creating a number of Education Investment Areas (EIAs). These are reminiscent of the Education Action Zones (EAZs) of the past.

Information point: EAZs, OAs, and EIAs

Education Action Zones (EAZs)   These were launched in 1998 as a way of uniting businesses, schools, local education authorities (LEAs), and parents to modernise education in areas of social deprivation. They were considered to represent a third way in education.

Opportunity Areas (OAs)   Twelve OAs were formed in October 2016, as part of the government's approach to increasing social mobility. They include urban, rural, and coastal areas. Each one has a partnership board, working with the DfE's local delivery teams. Local priorities vary, but cover early years, primary and secondary education, post-16, and employment outcomes.

Education Investment Areas (EIAs)   These were announced in the Levelling Up White Paper. The 55 areas identified include 24 described as "High Priority EIAs". These are formed from the 12 existing OAs; a further 12 areas identified as also having low achievement and high levels of deprivation; and others seen as having the highest potential for rapid improvement.

The DfE's expectation is that multi-academy trusts (MATs) will expand into these areas. Other suggestions include helping more children from disadvantaged backgrounds to get into leading universities and opening new 16–19 free schools in the high priority EIAs.

Before moving on to look at the Skills Mission, there is a recognition that factors beyond the classroom impact on a child's potential. Mention is made of expanding the "Supporting Families Programme" (formally known as the "Troubled Families Programme") and investing in creating a network of Family Hubs.

Information Point: Children's Centres and Family Hubs

Under the last Labour government, Sure Start Children's Centres were introduced, catering mainly for families with children under five. They were opened first in the most deprived areas. At one time, there were 3,500 Children's Centres. Following a change of government, the number of these centres decreased and the words Sure Start were often dropped.

Under the present government, a Family Hubs Transformation Fund was launched to support the development of Family Hubs, building on the idea of children's centres but giving them a wider brief. In October 2021, the government announced that 75 upper-tier LAs would receive funding to develop Family Hubs and a further 12 LAs received funding as the result of their bids.

The Levelling Up White Paper filled in further details about Family Hubs, giving them scope to support families with older children as well as the under-fives. This means providing services for young people and their families up to the age of 19, or to 25 if young people have special educational needs and/or disabilities.

On its dedicated website, the Anna Freud National Centre for Family Hubs makes the point that, whatever they are called, the key point here is the need for services to work together, and, where possible, to be physically co-located. For example, The Family Hubs Network explains that one measure of a Family Hub working well, is when a family need tell their story only once and not have to repeat it to the different professionals involved. This is easier to achieve if they are in close contact with each other. In order to make the most of places that already exist, Family Hubs may, for example, be former children's centres; health centres; co-located with other services; in a community building or school; or they may be virtual.

The next mission to be covered is to do with increasing the number of young people with the technical skills to secure a good job, having gained the necessary qualifications. Much of this section of the Levelling Up White Paper is based on ideas in *Skills for Jobs: Lifelong Learning for Opportunity and Growth*, which was mentioned earlier. As a result of this white paper, employer-led "Local Skills Improvement Plans (LSIPs)" were introduced. Subsequently, LSIPs were placed on a statutory footing by the Skills and Post-16 Education Act 2022. Alongside this development, the government mentions its intention to reform the funding of further education (FE) to make it fairer and more straightforward, as well as setting aside additional funding for a Further Education Capital Transformation Programme. (Chapter 7 of this book has further information on funding).

The last of the four missions to be discussed is the one on Healthy Life Expectancy (HLE). Although focusing mainly on adults, some of what is said about this mission is applicable to the younger generation as well. The recent setting up of the Office for Health Improvement and Disparities (OHID) is mentioned, which is part of the Department of Health and Social Care (DHSC). The shift is towards preventing ill health rather than concentrating on treating people once they are ill. Also under the health mission, there is reference to NHS England rolling out social prescribing in line with the NHS's Long Term Plan. There is further information about the Long Term Plan and social prescribing in Chapter 4 of this book. At the end of the Levelling Up White Paper, there are two pages on each of the regions showing what is being planned and the funding that has been allocated. Clearly laid out with maps and photographs, this would make a very useful resource for many school subjects. Information on developments in Northern Ireland, Scotland, and Wales are also featured.

The final chapter of the Levelling Up White Paper refers to the UK government bringing forward legislation to put in statute some of the key pillars of its Levelling Up framework. This is being done through the Levelling Up and Regeneration Bill currently going through parliament. Levelling Up directors are due to be appointed to act as a bridge between local leaders and central government.

The Levelling Up and Regeneration Bill

In the wake of the white paper, on 11th May 2022, the Levelling Up and Regeneration Bill was introduced in Parliament and is wending its way through the various stages a Bill goes through in both Houses of Parliament. Although they are not mentioned individually, Part One of the Bill is devoted to the Levelling-Up missions, including an annual report of their progress as part of the legislation.

The Schools White Paper

Opportunity for all: strong schools with great teachers for your child, was presented to parliament on 28th March 2022, a month after the Levelling Up White Paper appeared and a day before the appearance of the SEND Green Paper. In his foreword to the Schools White Paper, Nadhim Zahawi, secretary of state for education at the time, wrote:

> My vision for this white paper and the SEND Review alongside it is simple: to introduce and implement standards that will improve children's education, deliver the right support if they fall behind and give them the tools to lead a happy, fulfilled and successful life.

The words Nadhim Zahawi uses are interesting. Firstly, because they show a very clear link between the White and Green Papers. Secondly, he uses the phrase "falling behind". This has been repeated in other documents, which never seem to differentiate between those pupils who have had temporary setbacks and, with extra support, may catch up, from those where extra support may be needed in the longer term and even then, they may not "catch up".

In the introduction to the Schools White Paper, the exact wording of the Levelling Up mission about education is repeated, but, as well as talking about 90% of primary children reaching the expected standard, a second part has been added about increasing the average GCSE grade in English language and maths from 4.5 to 5. The use of terms such as "expected standards" and "average grades" is discussed further in Chapter 6 of this book as not being inclusive language.

Contents of the Schools White Paper

Running to 60 pages, the Schools White Paper has four main chapters:

1. An excellent teacher for every child
2. Delivering high standards of curriculum, behaviour, and attendance
3. Targeted support for every child who needs it
4. A stronger and fairer school system.

The first chapter covers what has already been done to ensure teachers have the training and support they need, as well as summarising what more there is to do. This is shown by an illustration of what is called the "golden thread of teacher development" showing what is, or is becoming, available at each stage of a teacher's career. This will include some new National Professional Qualifications (NPQs). The stages of a teacher's career are divided as follows:

Trainee teachers
   Initial Teacher Training (ITT); core content framework
Early career teachers
   Early career support; early career framework (ECF)
Experienced teachers and middle leaders
   Specialist development; specialist NPQs
Senior leaders, heads, and executive leaders
   Leadership development and NPQs

The revised ITT Core Content Framework and the ECF are said to have been designed around how to support all pupils to succeed, including those with SEND. However, it does not go into any details about the kinds of conditions children may have or the range of approaches that might help them.
   Moving on to more experienced teachers, the specialist NPQs are:

- Leading Teacher Development
- Leading Teaching
- Leading Behaviour and Culture
- Leading Literacy

At the senior leadership level, NPQs are:

- Senior Leadership
- Headship
- Executive Leadership
- Early Years Leadership
- SENCO NPQ

The last of these is one of the consultation questions in the SEND Green Paper and is discussed in the next chapter. Establishing a National Institute of Teaching as a teacher development provider is mentioned, and work started in September 2022 as planned.

Moving on to the second chapter, plans are outlined for a new curriculum body to work with teachers in co-designing digital curriculum resources and video lessons, along the lines of the Oak Academy, which was set up during the pandemic to provide online materials for pupils having to work from home. The chapter goes on to say that:

> As part of a richer school week, all children should be entitled to take part in sport, music and cultural opportunities. . . The government will publish updated plans to support sport and music education in 2022, and will publish a cultural education plan in 2023, working with the Department for Digital, Culture, Media and Sport and Arts Council England.
>
> (Paragraph 64)

As well as introducing an NPQ in Behaviour and Culture, the government promises updated behaviour in schools guidance and the statutory suspension and permanent exclusion guidance. These have now been produced and are discussed in Chapter 5 of this book. In terms of supporting children's safety and wellbeing, in May 2022 an Implementation Plan was published in the wake of the 2017 *Transforming Children and Young People's Mental Health Provision – a Green Paper*. The Implementation Plan is described as a collaborative programme by the DHSC, the DfE, NHS England (NHSE) and NHS Improvement (NHSI) with support from Health Education England and the OHID. The plan gives an update on the rollout of Mental Health Support Teams and the number who have accessed the training for Senior Mental Health Leads. The Schools White Paper talks about speeding up this vital work, which will not be a moment too soon, particularly in the aftermath of a pandemic.

The third chapter of the Schools White Paper introduces the phrase that is used for the title of SEND Green Paper:

> we sometimes miss the needs of children who do not acquire the label of having SEND, or being disadvantaged. We need to pivot to a system where all children receive the right support, in the right place, at the right time.
>
> (Paragraph 90)

As well as the overlap between the Schools White Paper and the SEND Green Paper which was published the next day, there is a reference to *The **Independent Review of Children's Social Care***, which was published in May 2022. In addition, plans for more places are mentioned in terms of those needing either specialist or alternative provision. The chapter talks about the "Parent Pledge", which is a promise from government that any child who "falls behind" in English or maths will receive additional support, whether or not they have SEND. The lack of a description as to which children this covers leaves the phrase open to interpretation, but light thrown on this subsequently suggests that the extra support schools already provide, combined with the National Tutoring Programme (NTP), may largely cover it. If this proves to be the case, whether this will meet parental expectations remains to be seen. (The NTP is explained further in Chapter 7 of this book.)

The fourth and final chapter of the Schools White Paper mentions the 55 EIAs introduced earlier in the Levelling Up White Paper, in terms of the need for the schools in EIAs to join MATs. It is stated that a "messy" school system of LA schools and trusts has resulted in overlapping responsibilities. The stated ambition is for all schools by 2030 to have joined, or be preparing to join, what are termed "strong multi-academy trusts".

Information point: The Academies Programme (including free schools)

2002   First wave of academy schools introduced by the Labour government aimed mainly at given struggling schools greater autonomy.

2010   Conservative-Liberal Democrat Coalition government passed the Academies Act. The following year, the first 24 free schools appeared as a new type of academy. There have been many more since.

2017   With the growth of academies, MATS became the government's preferred model, although some were considered to have grown too large. Single-school academies were encouraged to join MATs.

2022   The Schools White Paper suggested LAs might be able to establish MATs. This was confirmed in May 2022, when guidance was published on LAs setting up MATs in areas where too few strong MATs already exist.

Previously, there had been a sharp divide between schools maintained by the LA and academies funded directly from government. Although the government wants a less "messy" system, where all schools would be academies or heading that way by 2030, they are keen to reassure LAs that their future, although different, is secure.

> Local authorities will remain at the heart of the system, championing all children in their area – especially the most vulnerable – as they step back from directly maintaining schools into their new role. In this role, they will harness their unique capacity to coordinate across local services to improve outcomes for children.
>
> (Paragraph 151)

In explaining the difference between the Schools White Paper and the Schools Bill, which is discussed next, the DfE wrote that, in tune with its Levelling Up agenda, it was a Bill *"to underpin the government's ambition for every child to receive a world-class education, no matter where in the country they live"*. At the same time, the DfE pointed out that there were elements of the white paper that did not need legislation and so would not be in the Bill. These included the Parent Pledge, a new curriculum body, and EIAs.

The Schools Bill 2022/23

When it was launched, it was described as a Bill about:

- The regulation of academies
- School and local education funding
- The attendance of children at school
- The regulation of independent educational institutions
- Teacher misconduct; and for connected purposes.

Starting its passage through Parliament in the House of Lords, it was not long before it had entered stormy waters. The Schools Bill is in five parts which mirror its original description.

The Bill introduces 15 new laws, which are mainly about changing some of the current laws covering academies, although these seem unlikely to survive even if the Bill itself goes through.

On 23rd May, at the second reading of the Bill, Lord Baker, education secretary between 1986 and 1989, warned that the bill *"increases the powers of the secretary of state and the DfE in a way unprecedented since 1870"*.

Baroness Morris, who served as education secretary from 2001 to 2002, said,

> The proposals in the bill on academies are incredibly tight. If you look down the list of powers which the secretary of state is taking to himself, they cover absolutely everything, from governors to the length of the day to the term to the curriculum.

Lord Knight, who served as schools minister in the Blair and Brown Labour governments, said the government's *"solution is jaw-dropping. . . making the secretary of state effectively the chief education officer for 25,000 schools"*.

After running into opposition from many sides, by June, Nadhim Zahawi, Education Secretary at the time, agreed to scrap or amend some of the clauses that were the most contentious. By the time of the third reading, the Bill had gathered more than 170 amendments, and was described as having to be "either gutted or scrapped". Following this, the next stage of the Bill was postponed, leaving it unclear whether or not the government might withdraw the Bill altogether. A further complication was the change of prime minister and uncertainty about where the Schools Bill might come in a different prime minister's order of priorities. At the same time, it is not known if the current secretary of state for education, Gillian Keegan, might want to get a diluted version of the Bill out of her in-tray, or if she might prefer to concentrate on seeing schools through a funding crisis made worse by the current steep rise in inflation.

If the Schools Bill does become an Act in some form of other, the desire for all schools to be part of MATs is unlikely to change. More productive would be for the government to recognise that some schools may prefer to remain in the partnerships, trusts, or federations they have already established, than spend time and money on thinking about new structures. The Bill also delivers on the government's commitment to move to a direct National Funding Formula (NFF), so that schools receive funding on the same basis, wherever they are in the country. However, trying to distribute funding in a similar way is not easy as it has to reflect the fact that every child, school, and area is different. (The NFF is discussed further in Chapter 7 of this book.) Earlier in this chapter, the Skills and Post-16 Act 2022 was discussed. This chapter ends with information about Careers Education and a conversation with Tracy Noble.

Careers Education

Since the 2011 Education Act, schools have had the responsibility of ensuring they secure independent careers advice, rather than local authorities continuing to be responsible. To assist them, the government established a National Careers Service and set up the Careers and Enterprise Company (CEC). The latter helps schools to implement the Gatsby Benchmarks.

Information point: Gatsby Benchmarks

- Developed in 2015, there are eight benchmarks for measuring an effective careers programme:
  1. A stable careers programme
  2. Learning from career and labour market information
  3. Addressing the needs of each pupil
  4. Linking curriculum learning to careers
  5. Encounters with employers and employees
  6. Experiences of workplaces
  7. Encounters with further and higher education
  8. Personal guidance

Two editions of *The SEND Gatsby Benchmark Toolkit* are designed for young people with SEND in all settings, including mainstream specialist and alternative provision.

Another significant development were the Careers Hubs, first piloted through the Local Enterprise Partnerships (LEPs) from 2015 and established from 2018.

Information point: Careers Hubs

In 2018, the first wave of 20 Career Hubs was established, followed by a second wave of 18 more hubs in the following year. Each hub brings together a group of up to 40 schools and colleges to improve careers support for young people in their area.

> By bringing schools and colleges together with universities, training providers, and employers, expertise can be shared and careers education is more likely to be able to give young people the information they need, in order to know the choices available to them and make the most of their talents.
>
> The NE LEP has a regional College Hub, serving nine FE colleges and one sixth form college. In addition, it has one of two SEND Hubs – the other is in Leeds. They will support making the Gatsby Career Benchmarks relevant and effective for SEND learners.

An amendment to the Technical and Further Education Act (2017), known as "The Baker Clause" after Lord Baker (a previous secretary of state for education) stipulated that schools must allow colleges and training providers access to students in Years 8 to 13 to inform them about approved technical education qualifications and apprenticeships. Amanda Spielman, His Majesty's Chief Inspector, later commented that Ofsted would always report a school that failed to comply with the Baker clause, and that it would be unlikely for a school to be seen as outstanding if this were the case. Ofsted's school inspection handbook has been updated to highlight the importance of schools understanding and meeting the requirements of this legislation, which is one of the key areas that informs inspectors' overall judgements on Personal Development.

At the time of writing, the latest careers guidance is: *Careers guidance and access for education and training providers – Statutory guidance for schools and guidance for further education colleges and sixth form colleges*. Although published in July 2021, the guidance does not take effect until September 2023. In it, the DfE points out that its reforms to technical education and skills, as well as the impact of COVID-19 on the labour market, means that there is

> an increasing need for schools and colleges to work in partnership with employers, careers advisers, LAs and other education and training providers, to support students to prepare for the workplace and to make informed choices about the next step in their education or training.

Although this book is concerned with the importance of closer working across the services of education, health, and social care, throughout the chapters other forms of partnership working are seen as being an integral part of maximising young people's opportunities and improving their outcomes.

Timeframe Careers advice and changes

2011   **Education Act** changes how careers guidance services are provided.

2012   National Careers Service established as a resource.

2015	Careers and Enterprise Company supports schools and colleges through providing resources, including developing the Gatsby Benchmarks.
2015–17	Local Enterprise Partnerships pilot Careers Hubs, which were further developed in the next two years.
2017	Technical and Further Education Act included the Baker clause.
2021	The White Paper, Skills for Jobs: Lifelong Learning for Opportunity and Growth leads to the Skills and Post-16 Act.
2022	Education (Careers Guidance in Schools) Act passed which extends Careers Education throughout the secondary phase.
2023	Updated Careers Guidance published.

After several upheavals in terms of how careers advice has been given to pupils over the last decade, it is encouraging that greater attention is again being paid to giving young people the information they need to guide them in the choices they can make while still at school, as well as the routes into education, training, and employment once they leave. In the same way that a fixation on getting more and more people into university is starting to change into an acknowledgement that FE can suit some students better than HE, and T Levels could become established as a valuable alternative to A Levels, there is a recognition that pupils need a variety of paths once they move on from school. The following conversation is with Tracy Noble, who had years of experience as a trained careers adviser in a number of roles before devoting her skills to supporting young people with learning difficulties and disabilities.

In conversation with Tracy Noble, Team Manager for Hertfordshire's Learning Difficulties and/or Disabilities (LDD) Team of Services for Young People

Q. Could you describe your current role and the experience you gained which led up to it?

A. I took a circuitous route to where I am today. I came to it via biochemistry and physiology, followed by a PhD in population genetics which involved getting to grips with IT. I loved the research and the science part of the job, but realised that I liked working with people more. So, after working for an IT company and finding I liked training people, I decided to go into teaching. I thought about qualifying to work in further education (FE), but then chose to train at Birmingham City University as a careers adviser. I enjoyed this more than anything I'd done before. I completed the Diploma on the job by working at a huge comprehensive school. I used to arrive at 8 am every day and there would be students waiting for me who wanted to talk to me and get advice about what they should do next.

Then I was asked to take on a group of boys in Year 10 whose behaviour meant they were unlikely to make it into the sixth form. Although they weren't easy to manage, I loved it and when my assessor, who supported a group of special schools in Northants, went on maternity leave, she asked me to fill in for her. After that, I trained to be a special needs adviser and picked up a job in Hertfordshire. When a team leader's job came up, I applied for it and got it. I realised then how much I liked working with young people with SEND and being part of a team, so when the Team Manager's job came up I applied for it and I've had this role ever since.

Q. Could you say something about which young people are covered by the term "LDD"?

A. Although I've been in the same role for many years, there have been several reorganisations resulting in changes. Currently, I have a team of 12 Personal Advisers and we work with young people between the ages of 13–25 who have EHC plans. My team works with a whole range of needs, from those in mainstream settings to young people who have profound and multiple learning difficulties (PMLD).

Q. Do you work with many who are children in care, fostered, or have been adopted?

A. My team has been commissioned by the Virtual School Head to provide additional careers guidance to children in care who are in Year 11 in special schools in the county and those with EHC plans who are educated in other LAs. My team also supports Care Leavers up to the age of 25, although when they reach the age of 21, it's up to them whether or not they want to be supported.

Q. Have you helped those described as "NEETs" to move out of that category?

A. Yes, LAs are required by government to keep in touch with these young people and to reduce the number who fall into this category. So we have a team of "Keeping in Touch" advisers who support young people to access job vacancies and refer them to Personal Advisers. There has been some lottery funding to mentor those who have multiple barriers to becoming employed, for example those who rarely leave their bedrooms, and Covid has made this worse.

Q. Do you work with the alternative provision sector?

A. Not directly, although we do have some contact with the sector. Unfortunately, there's a lack of funding for it from the Education and Skills Funding Agency, so there aren't many post-16 training providers.

Q. What do you think of the introduction of T Levels and the changes to Level 2 and below qualifications?

A. T Levels are a positive development and provide a good alternative for those who want something more vocationally based. Many students with SEMH, for instance, prefer something practical and hands-on rather than sitting in a classroom Something that gives more immediate gratification rather than working towards something longer term may appeal to many of them.

However, on the negative side, they aren't accessible for those in the lower ability range, such as MLD and below. It's the same with apprenticeships, they aren't made accessible either. More could be done but it would cost.

Q. What efforts do you see FE colleges making to provide courses for those who are less academic or may need a different approach to engage them in learning?
A. The colleges I work with are prepared to be flexible and to offer programmes that meet the needs of a variety of learners. They recognise that students who are autistic, for example, may use a different way of thinking and this should be valued.

Q. What do you see as the value of work experience, traineeships and supported internships?
A. My service is available to help special schools form links with businesses, so that pupils in Years 10 and 11 can gain some work experience while still at school. Although there is no requirement, I think it's critical, otherwise some of them may never have a chance to experience what it's like to have a job. Traineeships are often only about 20 weeks long and this may not be long enough for young people to find their feet. Supported internships can be very useful provided they lead to job opportunities. "Project Search", which started in America, has had some success in showing that some of the young people who might not previously have been considered capable of holding down a job have moved into work on a full- or part-time basis.

Q. Does your role give you much involvement with parents and carers?
A. This is critical to the work we do. In fact, we couldn't do it without the parents being on board. If the young person is operating at SLD/ PMLD level, parents can be an enormous support in assisting with communicating. If the parents aren't supportive, particularly when it comes to the possibility of employment, it may not happen. Some may have been told not to expect that their son or daughter will find something to do when they finish college and so they may be rather overprotective. But I believe almost everyone can achieve something in life and we've found that putting on courses for parents about moving into employment can overcome this concern.

Q. Do you work with colleagues from health and from social care and, if so, what does this involve?
A. Since the Children and Families Act 2014, the level of involvement from health and social care has increased. My team now works closely with local social care teams and has much more involvement with health than previously. Sadly, the difficulty in recruiting social workers and the essential use of agency staff sometimes makes it difficult to develop and maintain relationships.

Q. Do you think interagency working is improving?
A. I do and I'd like to network more, but we all suffer from a lack of time.

Q. As a school governor, how do you make a contribution to the Governing Board and what have you gained by being a governor?

A. Although I live 50 miles from the school where I'm a governor, I love it. It's been easier since some of the meetings have been online. I used to be the careers adviser at the school when I first came to Hertfordshire. I wanted to use my knowledge and experience to support the current children and young people being educated in the school.

Q. Is there anything else you'd like to add?

A. I am proud to lead a team of careers advisers and related staff who support some of the most vulnerable young people in our society, to help them find their place in the world.

References

Anna Freud – National Centre for Family Hubs (2022) Available from https://www.annafreud.org/clinical-support-and-services/national-centre-for-family-hubs/

DfE (2013) *Sure Start Children's Centres Statutory Guidance.* Available from https://assets.publishing.service.gov.uk/government/uploads/system/uploads/attachment_data/file/678913/childrens_centre_stat_guidance_april-2013.pdf

DfE/DoH (2017) *Transforming Children and Young Peoples Mental Health Provision, Green Paper.* Available from https://www.gov.uk/government/consultations/transforming-children-and-young-peoplesmental-health-provision-a-green-paper

DfE (2022a) *Policy Paper – Opportunity for All Strong Schools with Great Teachers for Your Child.* Available from https://www.gov.uk/government/publications/opportunity-for-all-strong-schools-with-great-teachers-for-your-child

DfE (2022b) *Transforming Children and Young People's Mental Health Implementation Programme.* Available from https://www.gov.uk/government/publications/transforming-children-and-young-peoples-mental-health-provision

Family Hubs Network (2022) Available from https://familyhubsnetwork.com https://resources.careersandenterprise.co.uk/resources/gatsby-benchmark-toolkit-send

Gov.UK (2010) *Academies Act.* Available from https://www.legislation.gov.uk/ukpga/2010/32/contents

Gov.UK (2015) *Gatsby Benchmarks.* Available from https://resources.careersandenterprise.co.uk/resources/gatsby-benchmark-toolkit-send

Gov.UK (2017) *Technical and Further Education Act – The Baker Clause.* Available from https://www.google.com/search?client=safari&rls=en&q=Technical+and+Further+Education+Act+(2017&ie=UTF-8&oe=UTF-8

Gov.UK (2021a) *Guidance – Family Hubs Transformation Fund.* Available from https://www.gov.uk/government/publications/family-hubs-transformation-fund

Gov.UK (2021b) *HMCI Commentary: Putting Children and Young People with SEND at Heart of Our Recovery Plans.* Available from https://www.gov.uk/government/speeches/hmci-commentary-putting-children-and-young-people-with-send-at-the-heart-of-our-recovery-plans

Gov.UK (2021c) *Skills for Jobs: Lifelong Learning for Opportunity and Growth.* Available from https://www.gov.uk/government/publications/skills-for-jobs-lifelong-learning-for-opportunity-and-growth

Gov.UK (2021d). *Statutory Guidance – Early Years Foundation Stage (EYFS) Statutory Framework.* Available from https://www.gov.uk/government/publications/early-years-foundation-stage-framework--2

Gov.UK (2022a) *Careers Guidance and Access for Education and Training Providers.* Available from https://www.gov.uk/government/publications/careers-guidance-provision-for-young-people-in-schools

Gov.UK (2022b) *Education (Careers Guidance in Schools) Act.* Available from https://bills.parliament.uk/bills/2895

Gov.UK (2022c) *Health and Social Care Act.* Available from https://www.legislation.gov.uk/ukpga/2022/31/introduction/enacted

Gov.UK (2022d) *National Professional Qualifications Frameworks from Autumn 2021.* Available from https://www.gov.uk/government/publications/national-professional-qualifications-frameworks-from-september-202

Gov.UK (2022e). *Policy Paper – Levelling Up the United Kingdom.* Available from https://www.gov.uk/government/publications/levelling-up-the-united-kingdom

Gov.UK (2022f) *Policy Paper Levelling Up and Regeneration Further Information Levelling Up and Regeneration Further Information.* Available from https://www.gov.uk/government/publications/levelling-up-and-regeneration-further-information/levelling-up-and-regeneration-further-information

Gov.UK (2022g) *Levelling Up and Regeneration Bill.* Available from https://bills.parliament.uk/bills/3155

Gov.UK (2022h) *Opportunity for All: Strong Schools with Great Teachers for Your Child.* Availablefromhttps://www.gov.uk/government/publications/opportunity-for-all-strong-schools-with-great-teachers-for-your-child

Gov.UK (2022i). *Schools Bill: Policy Statement.* Available from https://www.gov.uk/government/publications/schools-bill-policy-statements

Gov.UK (2022j) *Schools Bill.* Available from https://bills.parliament.uk/bills/3156

Gov.UK (2022k). *SEND Review: Right Support, Right Place, Right Time.* Available from https://assets.publishing.service.gov.uk/government/uploads/system/uploads/attachment_data/file/1063620/SEND_review_right_support_right_place_right_time_accessible.pdf

Gov.UK (2022l). *Skills and Post-16 Education Act 2022.* Available from https://www.legislation.gov.uk/ukpga/2022/21/contents/enacted, https://resources.careersandenterprise.co.uk/resources/gatsby-benchmark-toolkit-send

MacAlister, J. (2022) *Independent Review of Children's Social Care: Final Report.* Available from https://childrenssocialcare.independent-review.uk

NHS (2019) *NHS Long Term Plan.* Available from https://www.longtermplan.nhs.uk; https://familyhubsnetwork.com; https://www.nationalcentreforfamilyhubs.org.uk/

2 The SEND Green Paper 2022

An evolving SEND system

> We are proposing to establish a single national SEND and alternative provision system that sets clear standards for the provision that children and young people should expect to receive, and the processes that should be in place to access it, no matter what their need or where they live.
>
> (SEND Green Paper, 2022: 6)

The above quote comes from the ministerial foreword to the SEND Green Paper, signed jointly by the Secretaries of State for Education and for Health and Social Care. This chapter begins by looking at what led up to the latest developments in providing for children and young people who have special education needs and disabilities (SEND), as well as those who may need alternative provision (AP). This is followed by a detailed examination of the proposals in the green paper, *SEND Review: Right support, Right place, Right time*, and some of the reactions to it. The chapter ends with a conversation with Carol Kelsey, a parent with personal experience of having a child with SEND. She describes her work in helping other parents to find their way through the SEND system, partly due to her role with the National Network of Parent Carer Forums (NNPCF).

How the SEND system evolved

In the UK today, although there may still be heated debates about how and where children should be educated, there is no argument about all children and young people, regardless of age or ability, being included in the education system. Yet, as recently as the second half of the last century, there was little attempt to support all learners. Instead, it was accepted that some children were ineducable and placed under the care of the health service rather than being seen as the responsibility of education.

The Warnock Report and the 1981 Act

It was not until the 1970 Education Act was passed that all children were brought into the education system. A few years after this happened, Mary Warnock, later Baroness Warnock, was asked by the government to see what was happening to

DOI: 10.4324/9781003333203-4

these children. Her *Report of the Committee of Inquiry into the Education of Handicapped Children* was published in 1978 and its effects have been long lasting. It was members of Warnock's committee who decided to change the terminology from 'handicapped' to having 'special educational needs' (SEN).

The term SEN was also designed to cover a much wider range of children whose needs, while less severe, require additional support at some stage of their education. As this extended group amounted to around 20% of the pupil population, rather than just the 2% formerly described as "handicapped", there were concerns that those with the most significant needs might be overlooked. To guard against this, the 1981 Education Act which followed the Warnock Report put in place the statementing procedures. These existed until replaced in 2014 by Education, Health and Care Plans (EHCPs).

The first SEN Code of Practice

In 1993, a further Education Act specified that an SEN Code of Practice should be issued from time to time. The following year, **Code of Practice on the Identification and Assessment of Special Educational Needs** was published, to provide guidance to local authorities (LAs) and governing bodies of schools on their responsibilities towards pupils who have SEN. In addition, the code introduced the idea that every school should have a qualified teacher who would take on the role of special educational needs co-ordinator (SENCO). Later, it became mandatory for SENCOs, as well as being qualified teachers, to have an extra qualification, the National Award for SEN Co-ordination.

In 2001, the SEN and Disability Act (SENDA) led to a second version of the code, in order to recognise the changes brought about by this Act. It included the need for "reasonable adjustments" to be made, so that disabled children and young people would not be discriminated against, but would be included in activities alongside their non-disabled peers.

Information point: Reasonable adjustments and accessibility plans

Schools are expected to provide auxiliary aids or services for a disabled pupil, if such aids would alleviate any substantial disadvantages a pupil faces in comparison to non-disabled pupils, as long as it would be considered reasonable to do so.

Accessibility plans are designed:

- To increase the extent to which disabled pupils can participate in the school's curriculum
- To improve the physical environment of the school in order to help disabled pupils to take advantage of what the school offers

- To improve the delivery of information which is readily accessible to pupils who are not disabled.

Schools are not expected to make physical adaptations to the building in the shorter term, such as providing lifts, but accessibility plans should show how the school is planning to improve accessibility arrangements over time.

This approach originated from the Disability Discrimination Act (DDA), which was later superseded by the Equality Act (2010). The latter brought several pieces of legislation together.

Information point: Equality Act 2010

The Equality Act covered the need to eliminate discrimination; to advance equality of opportunity; and to foster good relations. This Act replaced other important pieces of legislation, including a large number of Acts and Regulations, such as:

The Equal Pay Act 1970
The Sex Discrimination Act 1975
The Race Relations Act 1976
The Disability Discrimination Act DDA 1995

The Employment Equality (Religion or Belief) Regulations 2003
The Employment Equality (Sexual Orientation) Regulations 2003
the Employment Equality (Age) Regulations 2006

In May 2014 the DfE produced advice for school leaders, school staff, governing bodies and LAs explaining their duties in terms of both "reasonable adjustments", and having accessibility plans, which have to be updated every three years.

Returning to the contents of the second code of practice, this was known simply as the *Special Educational Needs: Code of Practice*. In the Preface, Estelle Morris, who was one of the few secretaries of state for education to have been a teacher, stressed the need for working in partnership across the three services, but also across other organisations as well:

The Code of Practice ... covers the special educational needs provisions of the Special Educational Needs and Disability Act 2001 and provides a framework for developing the strong partnerships between parents, schools, LEAs, health and social services and voluntary organisations that are crucial to success in removing barriers to participation and learning.

This code outlined four broader categories of need:

1. Communication and interaction
2. Cognition and learning
3. Behaviour, emotional, and social development
4. Sensory and/or physical needs.

Although by this time, there had been two codes of practice, there had been no major review of SEN since the Warnock Report. It was not until there was a coalition government formed by the Conservative Party and the Liberal Democrats that the path to the 2014 SEND reforms began and led to a third code of practice.

The 2014 SEND Reforms

At that time, Sarah Teather, a Lib-Dem MP, held the post of Children's Minister which included SEN. She issued a Call for Views which was open for five weeks asking for thoughts about what should be in the government's SEN green paper. Launching it, she said:

I want to look at every aspect of SEN – from assessment and identification to funding and education. We need to strip away the cumbersome bureaucracy but ensure there is a better, more comprehensive service for families.

This was followed by a Green Paper and a four-month consultation period, which led to the passing of the Children and Families Act. To give an idea of how the whole process happened, a timeline is given showing how policy was shaped over the course of five years.

Timeline: The SEND Reforms 2014

Autumn 2010 — Call for Views on the contents of an SEN Green Paper

March 2011 — Green Paper, *Support and aspiration: a new approach to special educational needs and disability – consultation* (for 4 months)

May 2012 — Government's response to the Green Paper – *Support and aspiration: a new approach to special educational needs and disability – progress and next steps*

Feb 2013 — Children and Families Bill introduced in Parliament

Feb 2014 — Children and Families Act receives Royal Assent.

Jan 2015 — *SEND Code of Practice: 0–25 years* published.

April 2017 — Ofsted and the Care Quality Commission start to inspect every local area to see how the SEND Reforms are being embedded across the three services.

The Children and Families Act 2014

Part Three of the Children and Families Act picked up the legislative changes to the SEN system and can be summarised as follows:

- Having one SEND system from 0–25 years
- Replacing School Action and School Action Plus with SEN support
- Replacing statements with EHCPs and bringing personal budgets into education as part of this
- Greater involvement of children and their families
- Greater input from health and social care
- Schools to produce an SEN information report
- LAs to produce a local offer

Although Sarah Teather had hoped for a clearer and less bureaucratic system which embraced the greater involvement of children, young people, and their families in the decisions that affect their lives, and despite the time taken from inception to legislation, implementation was patchy and a great deal of bureaucracy remained.

The SEND Code of Practice 2015

Although this was the third code, it was the first one to have "Disability" in the title and it was published jointly by the DfE and the Department of Health, as it was called at the time. As well as greater recognition being given to disability, prominence was also given to a young person's mental health and wellbeing, as well as their physical health. While three of the broad areas of need remained the same, BESD (behaviour, social, and emotional development) became social, emotional, and mental health difficulties, or SEMH for short. This shifted the focus from looking at a child's behaviour to what may lie behind it and whether this might include a mental health issue.

Area SEND inspections by Ofsted and Care Quality Commission

To make sure the changes would be embedded, the DfE gave Ofsted and the Care Quality Commission the task of inspecting jointly each of the local areas. Although these were based on LAs, they were known as the area SEND inspections, as the boundaries for health authorities are not always coterminous with LAs. Over time, these inspections showed that over half the areas were underperforming and were required to produce a Written Statement of Action to show how they would address the areas identified as needing further development. While it is easy to be critical, and it may be correct to say that some areas failed to pay sufficient attention to SEND provisions, during this time not only was there a pandemic, but also a shortfall in both funding and staffing across the services, which made it harder for the services to meet their legal obligations.

Following a timeline for the process of getting new reforms in place, the next chart sums up changes to the SEN/D system up to the commencement of the latest round of reforms which started in 2019.

Timeline: The evolution of the SEN/D system

1970 Education Act	All children have the right to be educated.
1978 Warnock Report	Introduced the term *special educational needs*.
1981 Education Act	Introduced statementing procedures
1993 Education Act	Required an SEN Code of Practice to be published
1994 SEN Code of Practice	Outlined the role of the special educational needs co-ordinator (SENCO)
2001 SEN and Disability Act	Known as SENDA for short
2001 SEN Code of Practice	Included new rights and duties contained in SENDA
2010 Equality Act	Brought together other Acts including the DDA
2014 Children & Families Act	Part 3 of the Act covered new duties as regards young people with SEND
2015 SEND Code of Practice	The first Code to cover SEN and/or disabilities
2019 SEND Review	Announced in the autumn

The next part of the chapter looks at the lead up to the SEND review 2022, the reasons for it, what it involved, and what it hoped to achieve.

The 2022 SEND review

When, in the autumn of 2019, another SEND review was announced, many were surprised that it was happening relatively soon after the last review. Originally, it was even referred to as a "rapid review" which would not spend much time going over old ground and a report was due to be published by the end of 2020. In the event, December came and went as did other deadlines, until people began to wonder whether it would ever appear. However, the need for a review was brought home to the government by the National Audit Office (NAO) saying that "*The system for supporting pupils with SEND is not, on current trends, financially sustainable*". The Education Select Committee waded in with the results of its own SEND inquiry, saying: "*the weight of evidence is clear. The system is not working – yet. … Families are in crisis, LAs are under pressure, schools are struggling*". After the review had been announced, the House of Commons Public Accounts Committee (which examines the value for money of government projects, programmes, and service delivery), made the following comment: "*We remain to be convinced the Department has sufficient grip on what needs to be done to tackle the growing pressures on the SEND system*".

In the event, little happened over the first two years, partly due to civil servants being hived off to cope with the aftermath of Brexit, combined with the arrival of a pandemic. However, one of the events that did take place was a conference arranged by the NNPCF to find out what members thought needed to change. From this conference, these clear messages emerged:

- Listen to families and intervene early
- Make sure there is enough money and spend it well
- Align incentives for school and system leaders
- Increased accountability
- Right people, right knowledge, right skills
- Lifelong outcomes
- Co-production

Information point: National Network of Parent Carer Forums (NNPCF)

2011   NNPCF launched with funding from central government.
2013   NNPCF became a formally constituted group.

Its structure mirrors the nine regions of the DfE, and within this structure there is a network of over 150 local Parent Carer Forums, one in almost every LA in England.

The Forum's work is divided into four stages, which form a continuous cycle:

1. Listening to members
2. Creating a picture of national priorities
3. Working with partners to deliver change
4. Feeding this back to the membership

In February 2021, the DfE announced that funding would continue for the time being.

With the SEND review still apparently in limbo, in June 2021 an update was published: *SEND: old issues, new issues, next steps*. It ended with this sentence:

> The need for a tightly coordinated, well-led set of changes across education, health and social care, with the aim of securing the very best provision and outcomes for children and young people with SEND, could not be clearer.

A new school year and a fresh impetus

In September 2021, the government carried out a major reshuffle, which meant an almost entirely new DfE under a new secretary of state, Nadhim Zahawi, who had the unusual background of arriving in England from Baghdad as an eight-year-old with no English. A new SEND review team was formed and a National SEND Reference Group and SEND steering group were established. The latter included different government departments; local government; representatives from parents, schools, colleges, early years providers, health, and care; and the voluntary and community sector. Their purpose was to assist the DfE in concluding the SEND review and to advise on proposals to be set out for consultation, which would be in the form of a Green Paper. The focus would be on improving outcomes for children and young people, to improve the experiences of their parents and carers, and to deliver reforms that would bring financial sustainability to the SEND system. This was no mean task.

Timeline: The SEND review

Sept 2019	Review announced
Dec 2020	Report expected, but delayed until early in the New Year
Jan 2021	Report delayed until Easter
Easter 2021	Report delayed until end of June
Sept 2021	New team starts work and report promised by end of March 2022.
March 2022	Report published in the form of a Green Paper. Consultation was to run until 1st July, but extended to 22nd July 2022.

The SEND Green Paper 2022

It was a surprise to find that, after the title on the cover: **SEND Review: Right support, Right place, Right time**, the title on the second page included the words: **Government consultation on the SEND and alternative provision system in England**.

This was the first indication that the proposal was to establish a single SEND and AP system. The number of pupils in AP settings who had diagnosed or undiagnosed SEND had grown substantially, so it was now a large majority.

Information point: Alternative Provision

Alternative provision (AP) comes in many forms, the best known of which may be Pupil Referral Units (PRUs). There are also AP Academies, including AP Free Schools, as well as:

- Hospital Schools and PRUs for children with medical needs
- Outdoor learning centres, forest schools, and therapeutic farms and centres
- Vocational and practical courses in various settings.

Pupils may attend full or part time, but if the latter, they must receive the equivalent of full-time education by combining more than one placement.

Widely known for supporting excluded pupils, or pupils at risk of exclusion, some APs cater for those who are school refusers; have medical needs, including mental health issues; or are waiting for a school place.

According to the Key Facts given in the SEND Green Paper, over 80% of pupils in AP have SEN, with nearly 80% of these pupils having SEMH as their primary need.

Some pupils are placed in unregistered provision, which is something the Schools Bill hoped to address.

The contents of the Green Paper

This 100-page document is packed full of ideas for setting up new systems and structures. It contains six chapters and while it would take too long to go through the contents of each chapter in detail, some of the content of each one is examined, along with the 22 consultation questions, which are woven through the chapters.

Chapter 1: The case for change

The first chapter does not include any of the consultation questions, but sets out the changes that are needed in order to reverse what is described as a "vicious cycle" of late intervention, lack of confidence in the system, and the inefficient use of resources, leading to:

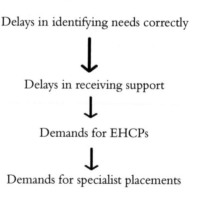

Delays in identifying needs correctly

↓

Delays in receiving support

↓

Demands for EHCPs

↓

Demands for specialist placements

The Green Paper suggests that this vicious cycle needs to be turned into a "virtuous cycle", with the services working together to ensure more children have their needs met in their local schools, without the need for an EHCP or a demand for specialist placements. However, at the end of the chapter, the government clarifies an inclusive system as being one where:

more children and young people able to have their needs met in high-quality mainstream provision. … We also need a strong specialist sector that supports those children and young people with more complex needs, and a clear vision for an improved alternative provision system that offers upstream support as well as placements.

(Paragraph 34 & 35)

Chapter 2: A single national SEND and alternative provision system

The first of seven consultation questions is based on the idea that the 2014 reforms placed such a strong emphasis on local decision-making that there are 152 local SEND and alternative provision systems. So, developing national standards is seen as the way to create consistency across education, health, and social care. To ensure the national standards are applied, local SEND partnerships would be established, convened by LAs and with representatives from early years, schools, further education (FE), alternative, and specialist provision, as well as partners from health and social care and from youth justice. They would produce local inclusion plans setting out what provision and services are available for SEND in that area.

National Standards ➜ Local SEND Partnerships ➜ Local Inclusion Plans

The first two consultation questions are as follows:

Consultation Question 1: *What key factors should be considered when developing national standards to ensure they deliver improved outcomes and experiences for children and young people with SEND and their families? This includes how the standards apply across education, health, and care in a 0–25 system.*

Consultation Question 2: *How should we develop the proposal for new local SEND partnerships to oversee the effective development of local inclusion plans whilst avoiding placing unnecessary burdens or duplicating current partnerships?*

The third consultation question looks at how LAs should commission services that go across LA boundaries. This is where regional and even national provision may need to be considered, for instance for blind, deaf, and deafblind pupils:

Consultation Question 3: *What factors would enable local authorities to successfully commission provision for low-incidence high-cost need, and further education, across local authority boundaries?*

The chapter moves on to consider EHCPs. There is no proposal to abandon EHCPs but to make them more effective:

Consultation Question 4: *What components of the EHCP should we consider reviewing or amending as we move to a standardised and digitised version?*

The fifth consultation question has been proving quite contentious. It is about parents and LAs working together to produce a "tailored list" of suitable placements, including placements in AP:

> Consultation Question 5: *How can parents and local authorities most effectively work together to produce a tailored list of placements that is appropriate for their child, and gives parents confidence in the EHCP process?*

The last two questions in this chapter seek to clarify LAs' dispute resolution and mediation services and make the latter mandatory before going to the SEND Tribunal. This is followed by a question on the role of the SEND Tribunal in terms of disability discrimination.

> Consultation Question 6: *To what extent do you agree or disagree with our overall approach to strengthen redress, including through national standards and mandatory mediation?*
>
> Consultation Question 7: *Do you consider the current remedies available to the SEND Tribunal for disabled children who have been discriminated against by schools effective in putting children and young people's education back on track?*

Chapter 3 Excellent provision from early years to adulthood

In looking at how to provide support from the early years onwards, the opening paragraphs clarify the need for a continuum of provision:

> An inclusive system will also ensure that children and young people have timely access to specialist services and support, including specialist placements where this is appropriate.
>
> (Page 37)

The first question suggests bringing together the information currently gathered by the Early Years Foundation Stage progress check for two-year-olds, and the Healthy Child Programme:

> Consultation Question 8: *What steps should be taken to strengthen early years practice with regard to conducting the two-year-old progress check and integration with the Healthy Child Programme review?*

Although no consultation questions are involved, the next part of the chapter is about supporting families through creating more Family Hubs; extending the Supporting Families programme; and increasing the number of respite places. These were referred to in the Levelling Up White Paper, as was the Levelling Up mission of 90% of pupils reaching the expected standard by 2030, which also receives a mention here. This leads on to the Parent Pledge in the Schools White Paper, which would provide additional support for pupils who "fall behind".

The only consultation questions at this point are two on changing the SENCO qualification, the first of which suggests making it one of the suite of National Professional Qualifications (NPQs).

> Consultation Question 9: *To what extent do you agree or disagree that we should introduce a new mandatory SENCO NPQ to replace the NASENCO?*
>
> Consultation Question 10: *To what extent do you agree or disagree that we should strengthen the mandatory SENCO training requirement by requiring that headteachers must be satisfied that the SENCO is in the process of obtaining the relevant qualification when taking on the role?*

After considering important information about how to improve quicker access to diagnosis and to specialist support from across the services, there are no consultation questions on this section, but, instead, the next returns to the drive towards academisation. Following the government's previously stated claim of all schools becoming academies by 2030, the question here is not about whether this a good idea, but about the composition of Multi Academy Trusts (MATs):

> Consultation Question 11: *To what extent do you agree or disagree that both specialist and mixed MATs should coexist in the fully trust-led future? This would allow current local authority maintained special schools and alternative provision settings to join either type of MAT.*

Moving through the age range, the chapter ends with a focus on FE, including transitions; preparation for adulthood; the Skills Bill (which is now the Skills and Post-16 Act); and a new Occupational Standard for FE teachers. There is reference to the work on simplifying the assortment of qualifications for this age group, including the ones for students working at level 2 and below, and the increase in traineeships which can help some SEND learners to move on to apprenticeships.

> Consultation Question 12: *What more can be done by employers, providers, and government to ensure that those young people with SEND can access, participate in, and be supported to achieve an apprenticeship, including though (through) access routes like traineeships?*

Chapter 4 A reformed and integrated role for alternative provision

There are four consultation questions relating to AP. The first of these is about what is referred to as a "new national vision" for AP using a three-tier system of support, although some will be working along these lines already:

1. Providing targeted support to pupils in mainstream schools whose behaviour disrupts learning
2. Having time-limited placements in AP where more intensive support is needed
3. Arranging transitions back to a different school or to post-16 placement.

Consultation Question 13: *To what extent do you agree or disagree that this new vision for alternative provision will result in improved outcomes for children and young people?*

The second consultation question is about improving stability over funding, which has been a real difficulty for AP providers in terms of future planning.

Consultation Question 14: *What needs to be in place in order to distribute existing funding more effectively to alternative provision schools to ensure they have the financial stability required to deliver our vision for more early intervention and reintegration?*

As there is no performance table for AP schools, it is proposed that a new national performance framework based on five key outcomes should be introduced. The five outcomes would be:

1.   Effective outreach support
2.   Improved attendance
3.   Reintegration
4.   Academic attainment, with a focus on English and maths
5.   Successful post-16 transition

Consultation Question 15: *To what extent do you agree or disagree that introducing a bespoke alternative provision performance framework, based on these five outcomes, will improve the quality of alternative provision?*

The final question is about keeping track of where pupils are, including whether unregistered provision is being used:

Consultation Question 16: *To what extent do you agree or disagree that a statutory framework for pupil movements will improve oversight and transparency of placements into and out of alternative provision?*

Chapter 5 System roles accountabilities and funding reform

A section on strengthening accountability for SEND within the health system mentions the DfE's work with the Department of Health and Social Care (DHSC) and the contents of the Health and Care Bill, (which is now the Health and Care Act 2022). The first of two consultation questions looks at how the use of technology could lead to better data sharing and enable the planning and delivery of SEND services to be measured:

Consultation Question 17: *What are the key metrics we should capture and use to measure local and national performance? Please explain why you have selected these.*

The second consultation question in this chapter is around the proposal for a new national framework of bands and tariffs. Although many LA use this kind of system already, banding would be based on the national standards. These would set out specific types of provision for different needs.

> Consultation Question 18: *How can we best develop a national framework for funding bands and tariffs to achieve our objectives and mitigate unintended consequences and risks?*

Chapter 6 Delivering change for children and families

The four final consultation questions start with a proposal for a National SEND Delivery Board to be established during 2022, bringing together the relevant government departments, as well as parents and representatives of local government, education, health, and care in order to hold partners to account for the development and improvement of the system. This is followed by a general question about implementing the proposals this time round.

> Consultation Question 19: *How can the National SEND Delivery Board work most effectively with local partnerships to ensure the proposals are implemented successfully?*
> Consultation Question 20: *What will make the biggest difference to successful implementation of these proposals? What do you see as the barriers to and enablers of success?*

The penultimate question covers how to transition from the present SEND system to the next one. The final question asks for any other comments. It is worth remembering that any consultation may not include the questions people would like to answer, so Question 22 is a timely reminder that it is not necessary to answer all the questions in a consultation, nor is there anything wrong in answering questions that have not been raised:

> Consultation Question 21: *What support do local systems and delivery partners need to successfully transition and deliver the new national system?*
> Consultation Question 22: *Is there anything else you would like to say about the proposals in the green paper?*

After reminding respondents that local areas are at different starting points, which have been exacerbated by the effects of the pandemic, one of the final paragraphs of the SEND Green Paper says:

> Equally, these proposals are not made in isolation but in the context of complementary changes to the education, social care, and health systems. We therefore want to seize this unique opportunity to deliver system-wide change for children and young people.
>
> (P.77: Paragraph 9)

Reactions to the SEND Green Paper

Although at the time of writing there has been no official response to the SEND Green Paper, a range of views are starting to emerge. One is based on this review being unnecessary as the proposals in the last review were sound and the necessary legislation is already there to make it happen. What went wrong was the way it has been implemented and the failure to hold people to account when legal duties have not been met. Another widely held concern is about a lack of information regarding how the changes would be funded. There is mention of money that has already been promised elsewhere and what other funding might be needed, but not about what new money will be injected into the system to kickstart any changes and to make it financially sustainable.

Other people have expressed a range of views. The DfE has indicated that it has received thousands of responses, so it will be some time before any further details are available. Will Quince, who was previously minister for school standards at the DfE and responsible for SEND, has been moved to the DHSC, which at least means he will still be involved in both health and social care. At the end of November 2022, Gillian Keegan, secretary of state for education, confirmed that a full response to the Green Paper would be published with an Improvement Plan early in 2023. Whatever the changes turn out to be, parents and carers will have a large role to play. This chapter ends with a conversation with Carol Kelsey, who was mentioned at the start of the chapter. She mentions her involvement with the NNPCF as well as with Short Breaks.

Information point Short Breaks/respite

Short breaks were established in 2008. They are designed to help those who are caring for a disabled child to have a break from their responsibilities. They also provide opportunities for the child to have a change of scene and experience different activities.

Short breaks can include:

- Children being looked after in their own home so carers have time to themselves
- Children being looked after away from home for a day, overnight, or for a longer residential stay
- Families being part of the Family Link scheme, where children stay with another family on an occasional or regular basis.

Since the Children and Families Act 2014, information about Short Breaks should appear as part of every LA's local offer.

Although LAs have a legal duty to provide Short Breaks for carers and disabled children, funding has been described as being patchy and from time to time there have been cutbacks to what has been available to parents and carers. This is another example of legal duties not always being matched by requisite levels of funding. However, after a campaign by the Disabled Children's Partnership (DCP), in February 2022 the DfE announced that funding would be available for the next three years to set up more than 10,000 additional respite placements.

In conversation with Carol Kelsey, NNPCF Eastern Region National Representative

Q. How long have you been involved with supporting parents of children and young people who have SEND and how did it come about?

A. I gave up my career working in the HR department of a business and as a teacher in the 1980s, in order to concentrate on the needs of my family, having become a parent/carer to my child with special needs. Later, I decided to turn my learning to good use, by helping other parents find their way through the SEND system. I became involved in HARC, which stands for Hertfordshire Autistic Resource Centre, and is the local branch of the National Autistic Society (NAS). I became a founding member of my local parent carer form in 2009 under the government Aiming High for Disabled Children programme, which focused on Short Breaks for disabled children and their families. Herts Parent Carer Forum, a Community Interest Company, is still thriving and I have represented the forum locally and regionally on many projects. In 2014, I became a national representative for the National Network of Parent Carer Forums and have represented parents on a number of national projects and groups.

Q. Since the SEND Green Paper was published, what have been parents' reaction to it?

A. Parents are people, so their views range from being deeply sceptical about the Green Paper, to seeing it as the answer to everything! There is scepticism about some of the proposals and concern about the possibility of legal rights being removed or watered down. However, much of it has been received positively and there are some good ideas in it.

At the present time, parents are still angry about the cost of living on top of a decade of cuts to services and it's likely to get worse before it gets better. While there's no shortage of data about disability, the effect on families of having a child with complex needs is often overlooked. For instance, having to go from both parents being in work to one having to stay at home and the family budget being much smaller.

Q. What are you own views on whether or not the Green Paper is likely to be successful in improving the lives of children with SEND and their families?

A. Personally, I think good things could come from it, but as it's a Green Paper, it depends on the detail; what emerges at the end of the process; and then on how the changes are implemented. Accountability is not tight enough at the moment, with LAs, and sometimes schools, not complying with the law, but no one does anything about it. There is nothing in the document about helping parents to understand either the SEND system or their own child's needs. This could be done by having a national offer, which would set out the expectation of what should be happening in each local area and what parents can expect from the LA and from schools. It would include information about how much money schools have received for SEND and be on every school's website, so that parents couldn't be told there's no money for SEND, but they would have clarity about how much there is and how it's being spent. This happens already for pupil premium money, but not for SEND. Parents can't be effective advocates for their children with SEND, if there's not enough clarity about what schools and what LAs should provide.

It's disappointing that both ITT [initial teacher training]and CPD [continuing professional development] remain weak on SEND. More needs to be done, including how to address pupils' needs and how to speak to parents about their child. It doesn't give me much confidence when the Green Paper continues to talk about what _all_ children should be aiming for. Where is the evidence that 90% of children should be able to reach a certain level of reading at a set age by 2030? And what is the impact on all pupils when this is seen as the aim for everyone?

Q. Do you have a view on whether or not it is helpful to talk about SEND and AP being part of one system?

A. This is a tricky one, as AP covers such a range of providers. Some sit outside being Ofsted-registered. Admittedly, PRUs, for example, have a high percentage of pupils with SEND, but do all the staff there know how to meet their needs? Do local areas know which type of provision will best meet the needs of pupils where mainstream education isn't the answer? I know of teenage girls who have been out of school, but have been able to return after having a time looking after horses through an AP provider. Both AP and special schools have a part to play in providing outreach, which is essential for supporting early intervention and to help untangle a child's difficulties as soon as possible.

Q. Do you think Family Hubs will turn out to be an improvement on children's centres?

A. This depends on how well the concept is thought through; how they are set up; and the funding they attract. The fact that they cover a wider age range and provide a broader range of services is to be welcomed, but finding the workforce may be a problem. TAs [teaching assistants] and office staff, for instance, are proving hard for schools to find as well as teachers.

The fact that Family Hubs put a greater emphasis on SEND is helpful. In Herts, they are called Family Centres. Some are based on children's centres and concentrate on Early Years, while other have moved on to be more like Family Hubs.

Q. What are your thoughts on the government's Parent Pledge, that any child will be given extra support if they fall behind?

A. This sound to me like a gimmick. Many children with SEND underperform despite being in the normal cognitive ability range because people don't always know how to help them. Some of them may know more than their teachers, for example in being able to manipulate IT systems, but can be punished for not doing what they are asked to do, rather than being rewarded for their ingenuity, such as the pupil who changed all references to the head teacher on the school's website to Shrek! Will whoever provides the extra tuition have the skills and techniques to bring on those who are described as falling behind? Better teacher training and CPD would give teachers the right skills instead of relying on tutors to understand a pupil's needs. In any case, we may have the wrong expectations of pupils who are referred to as "falling behind".

Q. What has been your experience of working across the services of education, health, and social care?

A. The real issue here is that they don't really understand how each other operates. In a sense, children's social care is the poor relation in terms of SEND. The training social workers receive doesn't usually prepare them for anything beyond understanding their role in safeguarding and knowing about attachment disorder, but not about working with the whole range of SEND children and young people, as well as with their families. Thresholds are getting higher for gaining access to services and this increases the pressure on parents who feel anger that, for example, 'short breaks' have become so short that they might be just a couple of days in the holiday period. Although there is a proposal in the Green Paper for social care to have a role like there is for health, where most local areas have either a Designated Medical Officer or a Designated Clinical Officer, but, as yet, there's no equivalent.

In some LAs, the director of children's services is also responsible for adult social care, which makes it a very wide brief. In other areas, difficulties arise when children have to transition to adult health or social care, for instance at 16 or 18 years of age or later. There is often a lack of planning to help them through the period of transition.

All too often, on EHC plans, social care just put: "*Not known to this service.*" Sometimes it means that there has been a lack of funding to carry out an assessment. However, in some ways, I've found those working in social care have been more receptive than staff in education.

In the NHS, 65% of the funding goes on adults, particularly the elderly, and the health needs of children with more complex conditions aren't often dealt with locally, but in places like Great Ormond Street, so local links become tricky. As adults, they have to transfer from being under a paediatrician, to their health needs transferring to a range of specialists, for instance, one for heart problems, one for diabetes, etc. This makes it difficult to know who is responsible for what and who pays for it. Health are sometimes slower to put reforms in place and COVID hasn't helped. There is a huge workforce issue, too, and considerable variability in how far face-to-face appointments are offered.

Q. Many children with SEND and their families need the support of all three services. How do you think they might work more closely together and is this already happening to some extent?

A. Locally, a Down Syndrome Therapy Advice Clinic has been set up, where a physiotherapist, occupational therapist, and a speech and language therapist (SaLT), will be available at the same time for informal assessments and advice. Parents can refer their pre-school aged children directly to the clinic, which is really positive. There is also a trial running for parents of children aged 0–5 with complex health needs, which provides a key worker who can guide and support families through the SEND system as a whole and particularly help them manage the multiple appointments and services they are involved with. There are new developments on the horizon around clinics for children with autism and ADHD and setting up a neurodiversity hub. There have been a few problems when teachers don't agree that a child is autistic even if a health professional has said that they are.

It's disappointing that parents are still having to repeat the story about their child's needs, because the services don't share information enough. Parents of children who have complex needs are the ones who understand them best, but they don't get to see all the records that are held by the different services. The most practical way forward would be for parents and carers to be allowed to hold their own records, perhaps with support from a key worker where necessary. The question of using key workers hasn't been fully explored. They could be based in Family Hubs and be the link between the services.

There needs to be more of a shared vision across the services with a similar way of keeping records. SaLTs may deliver a series of six sessions and then, if the need is ongoing, parents have to put them back into the system and apply for further sessions. Counting the number of sessions delivered may not be the right measure. Likewise, GP data is inclined to be about bean counting rather than about the quality of the service.

I want to help make it possible for families of the future to have a better start for all children and we've lost our way a bit. The population isn't being replaced, so there are fewer children and we need all our children to be supported in functioning as well as they can and to get the best out of the lives they have.

This chapter has concentrated the SEND Green Paper. The following chapter is written in a similar way, but focuses on The independent review of children's social care.

References

DfE (2014) *The Equality Act 2010 and Schools. Advice for School Leaders, School Staff Governing Bodies and Look Authorities.* Available from https://www.gov.uk/government/publications/equality-act-2010-advice-for-schools

DfE (2022) *Policy Paper – Opportunity for All Strong Schools with Great Teachers for Your Child.* Available from https://www.gov.uk/government/publications/opportunity-for-all-strong-schools-with-great-teachers-for-your-child

DfES (1994) *Special Educational Needs. Code of Practice.* Available from https://assets.publishing. service.gov.uk/government/uploads/system/uploads/attachment_data/file/273877/ special_educational_needs_code_of_practice.pdf

Gov.UK (1970) *Education (Handicapped Children) Act.* Available from https://www.legislation. gov.uk/ukpga/1970/52/enacted

Gov.UK (1993) *Education Act.* Available from https://www.legislation.gov.uk/ukpga/1993/ 35/pdfs/ukpga_19930035_en.pdf

Gov.UK (1981) *Education Act.* Available from https://www.legislation.gov.uk/ukpga/1981/ 60/enacted

Gov.UK (1995) *Disability Discrimination Act.* Available from https://www.legislation.gov. uk/ukpga/1995/50/contents

Gov.UK (2001) *SEN and Disability Act (SENDA).* Available from https://www.legislation. gov.uk/ukpga/2001/10/contents

Gov.UK (2010) *Equality Act.* Available from https://www.legislation.gov.uk/ukpga/2010/ 15/contents

Gov.UK (2011) *Policy Paper: Support and Aspiration: A New Approach to Special Educational Needs and Disability – Consultation.* Available from https://www.gov.uk/government/ publications/support-and-aspiration-a-new-approach-to-special-educational-needs-and-disability-consultation

Gov.UK (2012) *Support and Aspiration: A New Approach to Special Educational Needs and Disability – Progress and Next Steps.* Available from https://dera.ioe.ac.uk/14455/

Gov.UK (2013) *Children and Families Bill.* Available from https://www.gov.uk/government/ publications/children-and-families-bill-2013

Gov.UK (2014a) *Children and Families Act.* Available from https://www.legislation.gov.uk/ ukpga/2014/6/contents/enacted

Gov.UK (2014b) *SEND Code of Practice: 0–25.* Available from https://www.gov.uk/ government/publications/send-code-of-practice-0-to-25

Gov.UK (2021) *Research and Analysis. Old Issues, New Issues, Next Steps.* Available from https://www.gov.uk/government/publications/send-old-issues-new-issues-next-steps/ send-old-issues-new-issues-next-steps

Gov.UK (2022) *SEND Review: Right Support, Right Place, Right Time.* Available from https://assets.publishing.service.gov.uk/government/uploads/system/uploads/attachment_ data/file/1063620/SEND_review_right_support_right_place_right_time_accessible.pdf

HMSO (1978) *The Warnock Report. Special Educational Needs.* London: H.M.S.O.

House of Commons Public Accounts Committee (2020) *Support for Children with Special Educational Needs and Disabilities – First Report of Session 2019–21.* Available from https:// committees.parliament.uk/publications/941/documents/7292/default/

House of Commons (2020) *Special Educational Needs and Disabilities (SEND): Education Committee.* Available from https://committees.parliament.uk/committee/203/education-committee/news/114698/special-educational-needs-and-disabilities-send-education-committee-publishes-government-response-to-report/

MacAlister, J. (2022) *Independent Review of Children's Social Care: Final Report.* Available from https://childrenssocialcare.independent-review.uk

National Audit Office (2019) *Support for Pupils with Special Educational Needs and Disabilities in England.* Available from https://www.nao.org.uk/report/support-for-pupils-with-special-educational-needs-and-disabilities/#

National Network of Parent Carer Forums. Available from https://nnpcf.org.uk

3 The Review of Children's Social Care 2022

Resetting the system

I am in no doubt that effective support for children and families cannot be achieved by a single agency acting alone. It depends on a number of agencies working well together. It is a multi-disciplinary task.

(Gov.UK, 2003: 1.30)

It is clear from previous chapters that there is much agreement that getting the three services to work more closely together is fundamental to improving outcomes for children and families. Whereas the last chapter focused on the SEND Green Paper, this chapter covers children's social care. It considers developments in children's social care leading up to the interim and final reports of the Independent Review of Children's Social Care (2022). As there were over 80 recommendations in Josh MacAlister's review, it is not possible to itemise them all in the same way that the 22 SEND Green Paper consultation questions were considered, but a flavour of each of the nine chapters is given and all the recommendations are listed in Appendix 2. The chapter ends with an insightful account by Richard Broadhurst from the perspective of someone who is both a social worker and an assistant head teacher. Social work has been around for more than a century and the British Association of Social Workers (BASW), which is the independent professional membership organisation for social workers, has helped to push through many of the reforms that have been made. In recent years, the demand for children's social care services has been rising. Local authorities (LAs) have received more money from the government, but this has not kept pace with demand. In addition, there have been difficulties in recruiting and retaining staff to work in social care.

How children's social care evolved

The current social care system started with the passing of the Children Act 1989, as amended. The Act established a number of key principles, including:

- The concept of parental responsibility
- The paramount nature of the child's welfare when a matter under the Act is before a court

DOI: 10.4324/9781003333203-5

- That children are best looked after by their family unless intervention in family life is essential.

The Act placed a general duty on LAs to promote and safeguard the welfare of children in their area by providing a range of services appropriate to their needs. It set out what an LA must do when it has reasonable cause to suspect that a child in its area is suffering, or is likely to suffer, significant harm. The Act sets out the circumstances under which a court may make an order placing a child in the care of the local authority; the functions of LAs in relation to looked after children (LAC); and a duty to safeguard and promote the welfare of children in their care.

Lord Laming's Inquiry

The next major impetus for change was the horrendous killing by her caregivers of Victoria Climbie, who was mentioned in the opening chapter of this book. Victoria was a young girl sent to this country to live with an aunt, in the hopes of receiving a better education. Her death led to a very thorough and damning report by Lord Laming. In his introduction he wrote that to say the relatives with whom she lived "*treated Victoria like a dog would be wholly unfair; she was treated worse than a dog*". The real tragedy was that Victoria was known to the services who might have saved her. A few days before her death, the house had been visited by a social worker, who, on getting no reply, went away assuming the family had moved. Meanwhile, Victoria was inside chained to a bath.

In his introduction, Lord Laming pointed out that this was not a case where a young child was not known. In fact, five social services departments; two hospitals; and two police child protection teams had been aware of her existence. In other words, it was not a question of lack of involvement, but the failure to build up a picture of what was happening through the information being shared.

Every Child Matters and the 2004 Children Act

Following Lord Laming's Inquiry, and, as mentioned in the Introductory Chapter to this book, the next major step was a Green Paper, **Every Child Matters**, which led to the Children Act. This stressed LAs' responsibility for overseeing the delivery of services for children and also for promoting their welfare and wellbeing. The importance of interagency working in terms of young people's safety and wellbeing has been understood for years, yet today, it does not always work in practice. There is a separate section in the Act giving the duties relating to Wales. In Scotland, these duties come under Health and Social Care Services and in Northern Ireland under the Health and Social Services Trust. The Children Act was followed in 2008 by The Children and Young Person's Act, which focused on improving the lives of children in care (CiC).

Information point: CiC/LAC and CiN

Children in Care (CiC) and Looked After Children (LAC)   These two terms are synonymous and refer to children who are likely to be living away from home. They may be in a children's home, with foster parents, or in a residential school setting. In Scotland, the term also includes those living at home who need regular contact from social services. LAC is said to be the term preferred by children and young people themselves who are in this situation.

Children in Need (CiN)   This term is not always used consistently. The broadest definition covers all those who receive support from a social worker, so it includes CiC/LAC, as well as all young people who are disabled. In some contexts, it may also cover those who have needed support from a social worker during the previous six years, are young carers, young asylum seekers, children whose parents are in prison, or who need support for their health or developmental needs. These are children who are likely to be living at home.

The most common reasons for children coming to the attention of social care services is due to domestic abuse, mental health difficulties, or substance misuse by parents. Children described as Children in Need (CiN) or LAC may be subject to a care order stating they are to be placed in LA care, or subject to a placement order which means they can be adopted. There is an extra layer of support for these children in the form of the virtual school head (VSH).

Information point: Virtual school head (VSH)

Since 2014, every LA has been required to appoint a virtual school head (VSH).

The VSH's role is to promote the educational outcomes of children aged 0–18 who have a social worker (SW) or have previously had a SW in the last six years.

In 2021, the role was extended to all those who had had a SW at some point.

VSHs do not work directly with individual children or their families, but have strategic leadership responsibility, which enables them to take an overview of the whole cohort of children within the LA.

Having one foot in education and one in social care, they act as a bridge between the two services.

The National Association of Virtual School Heads (NAVSH) is a charity run by a board of VSHs.

There is a helpline, Help at Hand, which is for children in care, those leaving care, those living away from home, or for those working with children's services. Free support, advice, and information is given to help tackle any challenges being faced (see website link at end of the chapter).

The Children and Social Work Act 2017

Returning to the next significant event, in 2017, the Children and Social Work Act was published. The Act had four main purposes:

- To improve decision-making and support for looked after and previously looked after children in England and Wales
- To improve joint work at the local level to safeguard children and enable better learning at the local and national levels to improve practice in child protection
- To promote the safeguarding of children by providing for relationships and sex education (RSE) in schools
- To enable the establishment of a new regulatory regime specifically for the social work profession in England.

The mention of children who had previously been looked after as well as those currently in care was later picked up through pupil premium funding to schools (see Chapter 7 of this book). The aim of providing RSE in schools did not come in until 2021, some of this delay being due to COVID.

Gradually, the organisation of services, the roles and responsibilities of all concerned, and the training for those who work in them has been improved. Sadly, however, the occasional, but still tragic deaths of children in their homes has continued to occur. While these hit the headlines and make some prospective social workers hesitate to take on this role, what is harder to measure are the times when families have been supported rather than a child taken into care; when foster carers have been found; and when children's lives have been turned round or even saved. These are the statistics that do not exist. It is an unfortunate fact that bad news soon spreads, whereas good news seems to be less widely noted.

The children in need review

In addition to Acts of Parliament, specific aspects of children's care are continually being refined. In December 2018, the DfE published the interim findings of a children in need review. The key points for action were addressed to all those who could help to put into practice what is needed. These were said to be: schools, social care, early help, health, the police, and unspecified others. In June 2019, the conclusions from the review were summarised in terms of the following areas for action:

- Visibility: the long-term effects of having short-term involvement with social care needs to be recognised and better sharing of information between social care and schools is needed

- Keeping children in education: the importance of regular attendance and avoiding exclusion is highlighted along with the role of Alternative Provision (AP)
- Aspiration: the emphasis should be on how to help these children succeed rather than lowering expectations; importance of VSH role
- Support in and around school: effective approaches and interventions should be shared more widely, so that schools can draw on a wider body of specialist support both within and beyond the school
- Supporting families and communities: this needs work across government departments to strengthen families and support them from early years to adolescence.

The CiN review suggested that both social workers and teachers need training to understand how these children's experiences may create barriers to learning. These may include: being unable to talk about what is happening to them; trying to concentrate on work when their mind is on other things; exhibiting challenging behaviour triggered by stress or confrontation; having worries about being bullied or stigmatised; or having SEND and attachment issues.

Training and roles

The difference between social care work and a social worker is that social workers need an honours degree to practise, whereas social care workers tend to offer more personal care, and in many cases do not require any qualifications when they start work as they are offered on-the-job training.

Social workers can either have a BA degree or an MA in social work. Experience is an important part of social work qualifications. A work placement forms half of social work courses, along with academic learning focusing on legislation, ethics, and theory. Some experience of social work or social care is needed when applying to study. This can be paid, voluntary, or placement work, or even life experience may count. There are nine stages of The Professional Capabilities Framework, which goes from entry right through to experienced, advanced, and strategic social worker.

Roles with children and families

Social workers may choose to work with a specific group of people such as adults, children, the elderly, families, or those with mental ill health, physical disabilities, learning disabilities, or alcohol and drug dependency. They may be employed by the NHS, schools, charities, or LAs. Wherever they work, the aim will be to care for and protect society's most vulnerable people. Employment opportunities in the social care sector as regards children can be grouped into:

- Childcare and early years
- Child protection
- Fostering and adoption

- Residential care
- Supporting independent living
- Youth and community work.

Working more directly with schools is something else that is beginning to happen.

Social Workers in Schools (SWiS) Project

One way in which social workers and teachers can learn from each other and joint working is strengthened, has been demonstrated by the Social Workers in Schools (SWiS) Project. This began as a small pilot in 2018–19 involving schools in Lambeth, Southampton, and Stockport. Since then, the project has been scaled up to embed 146 social workers in secondary schools in 21 LAs in England. A separate project as part of this work has been to provide supervision from experienced social workers to designated safeguarding leads (DSLs), which is running in 28 local authority areas.

It is not known how much longer there will be funding from the DfE to continue this promising development, but it is a step in the right direction in bringing the services closer together. The project has also shed some light on the need for those working in schools to have the kind of supervision long enjoyed by other professionals. This is particularly important since schools have become recognised for the work they do with pupils who have social, emotional, and mental health issues (SEMH).

In March 2022, a few months after he had been appointed Minister for Children and Families, Will Quince wrote an article about the vital work of social workers. He called them "unsung heroes". Recent figures suggest that there are nearly 40,000 child and family social workers in England, with around 20% of children having had the support of a social worker before their 16th birthday. Will finished his article by referring to "*eagerly awaiting The Independent Review of Children's Social Care*". A few months after he had written this, Will was moved from the DfE to become a Minister at the Department of Health and Social Care (DHSC).

Timeline: Some milestones in children's social care

1989	Children Act: LAs responsible for children's needs, including LAC
2003	Laming Inquiry led to Every Child Matters Green Paper
2004	Children Act: established LA Directors of Children's Services
2008	Children and Young Persons Act: about Children in Care
2017	Children and Social Work Act: including Relationships and Sex Education in schools
2018	Social workers in schools project
2018	Interim report: Children in Need Review
2019	Final report: Children in Need Review
2021	Interim Report: Independent Review of Children's Social Care
2022	Final Report: Independent Review of Children's Social Care

The Independent Review of Children's Social Care

Although the original intention had been to publish the SEND Green Paper and the outcome of Josh McAllister's review of children's social care at the same time, the latter was delayed until a national review into safeguarding had been published, following the murder in their homes of two more young children.

Following on from a commitment in the government's 2019 manifesto, on 15th January 2021 The Independent Review of Children's Social Care was announced and a former secondary school teacher, Josh MacAlister, was appointed as its chair. After teaching, Josh had set up a charity, Frontline, whose mission is, *"to create social change for children who do not have a safe or stable home, by developing excellent social work practice and leadership"*.

Early on after the review had begun, both a Call for Advice and a Call for Evidence were released. Also in its early stages, the National Network of Parent Carer Forums (NNPCF), whose work was explained in the previous chapter, met with the officials leading the social care review and raised the following five issues for the review team to consider:

- Support not safeguarding – much of the social care system is focused on safe-guarding when, what families need, is support.
- Input into EHCPs from social care – this is patchy and often doesn't happen or is superficial.
- Consistency and criteria – there is a postcode lottery for care services. Some recognise SEND children as CiN and some do not. There are different thresh-olds for services.
- Availability of services – these are not sufficiently available when needed. Thresholds and cuts have affected respite care, residential care, and Short Breaks
- Prioritisation with the NHS integrated care systems – children must be included in the plans for new integrated care systems.

As he promised when he took on the chairmanship, Josh MacAlister and his team worked at pace over the first three months, so they could publish an interim report by the summer. The review team concentrated on what was **not** working, in order to pose some questions before starting work on developing recommendations. After collecting information from many of those involved, four themes emerged:

1. Not enough help for families raising children in difficult circumstances, whether through poor housing or other problems faced by families.
2. Lack of effective intervention.
3. The system doesn't strengthen relationships and sometimes makes them worse.
4. The system as a whole is not improving.

Speaking on a YouTube video recorded on 24th June 2021 about this interim report, MacAlister told Mrunal Sisoda, joint chair of the NNPCF, that, although the review was not a SEND review, many of the themes resonate with SEND and there is a large overlap between the two reviews. Because of this, the work was being done in parallel and the two teams at the DfE were working closely together.

The interim report: *The Case for Change* (June 2021)

The report set out what needed to change in order to have an effective social care system for children and young people. The problems were set out as follows:

- More needs to be done to support families
- A more effective child protection system would mean more effective support and decisive action when required
- A care system should build rather than break relationships
- The rising cost of children's care results in money being spent on propping up an inadequate system rather than on longer-term investment in a better system.

Between the two reviews, in January 2022 the Children's Commissioner, Rachel de Souza, issued her own report: ***Children's Social Care – putting children's voices at the heart of reform***. In it, she explained that:

> While this submission inevitably focuses on challenges, it is vital to acknowledge that many children do have good experiences in care, and often have far better lives and outcomes than had they not received the love and support of their adoptive or foster family. A strong theme of our work is the appreciation of individual foster and adoptive parents, carers, and social workers, as well as teachers, and all other adults working with them.
>
> (P9)

The report pulls out four key things children and families need when in contact with social care:

- To be listened and responded to
- To have relationships that are trusting and stable
- To feel loved, supported and stable
- To be able to access practical help and support.

The report then offers a series of solutions for each of these key things:

1. Listening to children and families means ensuring they help to shape the care plans; have input into LAC reviews; and have some ownership of the process.
2. While there may be a plethora of people involved – the children, their social workers, birth and foster parents – children need at least one person they can turn to and trust. Social workers' caseloads need to be reduced and less frequent moves are a necessity. In addition, sibling relationships should be maintained if at all feasible.

3. Fewer changes in placements are essential for children's feelings of stability, which depend partly on ensuring enough placements are available. Where adoption is not a possibility, there should be the option of longer-term foster care, with a full leaving care plan for every young person.
4. Three areas of reforms are needed:
    i. Schools should become formal parts of safeguarding partnerships
    ii. In a similar way to education, health, and care plans, there should be integrated support from, in this case, the police, the NHS, and schools in delivering family services for children in care
       • Local safeguarding partnerships should have a common set of outcomes
       • Models of social prescribing within social care should be used to help social workers access key services for young people.

(Both safeguarding and social prescribing are considered in the next chapter of this book).

The final report of The independent review of children's social care

As promised, after two months delay in May 2022, **The independent review of children's social care – Final report** appeared. In his Chair's Foreword to the final report, Josh MacAlister wrote:

> The time is now gone for half measures, quick fixes or grandstanding. Changing the easiest bits, papering over the cracks, or only making the right noises, may in fact make matters worse. It will create the illusion of change but without the substance. It will dash hopes and fail another generation. That is why we have gone further than most reviews, not just saying what needs to change but also working through how and when change should be implemented.
>
> (2022a: 4)

Running to over 270 pages, the report has nine main chapters. Chapters 2–8 include over 80 recommendations. For those wishing to know more about the background to the recommendations, on the day the final report was published, **Recommendation Annexes – Additional detail on review recommendations** was released. This runs to over 200 pages and provides further background information on each of the recommendations.

Contents of The Independent Review

The headings of each chapter give an idea of the topics that are covered. There are no recommendations in the first and last chapters. In the other chapters, the recommendations are not numbered consecutively but start again for each chapter.

Chapter 1: Reset children's social care
Chapter 2: A revolution in Family Help (9 recommendations)

There are too many recommendations to list them all within these chapters, so, while the main themes are mentioned and a few of the recommendations quoted, all the recommendations are listed separately in Appendix 2 at the end of this book.

Chapter 1: Reset children's social care

In a similar way to the SEND Green Paper, the review talks about breaking a cycle of escalating need and crisis intervention and turning it into a virtuous cycle. This would mean shifting money and effort from reacting to crises to rebalancing resources to support families and others who care for children. So, instead of trying to fit children and families into the system that exists and maintaining the status quo, the system should be working in a way that meets their needs.

Chapter 2: A revolution in Family Help

The chapter introduces the term "Family Help", which is based on keeping families together whenever this is possible. It is designed to bring in and coordinate services and other partners to support families and prevent them falling between services, bringing early help to a wider group of families using a multidisciplinary approach. The director of children's services should oversee Family Help and Ofsted should be used to hold areas to account. The final recommendation in this chapter reads as follows:

> Government should ensure alignment in how the proposals in the SEND and AP Green Paper and this review are implemented. Government should ask the Law Commission to review the current patchwork of legislation that exists to support disabled children and their families.
>
> (P60)

Chapter 3: A just and decisive child protection system

The focus here is on improving the system for child protection. It is proposed that a new role of Expert Child Protection Practitioner should work alongside Family Help, where there are concerns of significant harm in connection with a family who is already known to the Family Help team. Other proposals include making it possible to have better information sharing between teachers, doctors, health visitors, neighbours, and the wider community, who are described as "the eyes and ears of the child protection system" (P80). Another recommendation is to add expectations about multi-agency working to the document, **Working Together to Safeguard Children**.

Chapter 4: Unlocking the potential of family networks

There is much in the review about the need to make better use of wider family networks. This chapter has a further eight recommendations on what needs to happen to support family members who are prepared to help out rather having to take children into care. This is often referred to as "kinship care". The place of foster and residential care is recognised, while pointing out that these alternatives come with an end date, whereas staying within the family may last a lifetime.

Chapter 5: Transforming care

This chapter is about transforming the care children receive both in children's homes and in foster care. A number of recommendations focus on replacing the myriad of complicated rules, guidance, and legislation with a new set of standards, which would set a high bar for the quality of care. These would need to be flexible enough "*to tailor homes around the hugely varied needs of children.*" The chapter goes on to highlight the need for more foster carers, which, in turn, means providing them with better support and more training.

Chapter 6: The care experience

This chapter is based on five missions which are said to be needed, if there is to be a dramatic change in how this community of children and their families are treated. The five missions are as follows:

1. By 2027, no young person should leave care without at least two loving relationships.
2. By 2026, double the proportion of care leavers should be attending university, and particularly high-tariff universities.
3. Also by 2026, at least 3,500 new well-paid jobs and apprenticeships for care leavers should have been created.
4. Reduce care-experience homelessness now, before ending it entirely.
5. Increase the life expectancy of care-experienced people, by narrowing health inequalities with the wider population.

As well as recommendations covering these issues, there are two on the role of VSHs. One proposes that VSHs should be accountable for the education attainment of children in care and care leavers up to the age of 25. The other one recommends that VSHs should identify more children in care who might benefit from a place at a state or independent day or boarding school, and the DfE should create a new wave of state boarding capacity led by the best existing schools.

Chapter 7: Realising the potential of the workforce

The question is raised of having a social work Early Career Framework covering the first five years (along similar lines to the one now in place for teachers). Turning round a situation where more time is spent on administration than being with children and families is addressed, as is the need to reduce reliance on agency social workers so that real relationships can be formed. There is a recommendation to train 700 more managers of residential children's homes, so that residential care can provide a specialised healing environment for the most vulnerable children.

Chapter 8: A system that is relentlessly focused on children and families

The 20 recommendations attached to this chapter include what is needed to under-pin the new system, including establishing a "National Children's Social Care Framework". Strengthening multi-agency working is also a key recommendation. Three other threads are around the funding of social care; improving the role of Ofsted to drive accountability; and making schools a statutory safeguarding partner.

Chapter 9: Implementation

The final chapter begins by summarising what each element of the proposals would cost. For those wishing to know more about the details, alongside the final report a technical report was released giving the cost-benefit analysis. Next, there is a timeline showing what needs to happen between 2022 and 2027. This includes a White Paper leading up to a Bill, followed by delivering on the recommendations between the spring of 2024 and 2027. By the end of 2027, the reforms should be in place and the children's social care system should result in more sustainable outcomes for children.

Responses to the final report

On the day the report was released, Will Quince gave an oral response to the report in Parliament. After thanking Josh MacAlister and all those who had supported him, he spoke of what his three priorities would be:

Firstly, to improve the child protection system so that it keeps children safe from harm as effectively as possible.

Secondly, to support families to care for their children, so that they can have safe, loving, and happy childhoods which set them up for fulfilling lives.

Thirdly, to ensure there are the right placements for children in the right places, so that those who cannot stay with their parents grow up in a safe, stable, and loving home.

He said that he would establish a National Implementation Board and he would work with the sector to develop the National Children's Social Care Framework and that details of this would appear before the end of 2022. He accepted in principle the suggested Early Career Framework to give more support to social workers early in their career and to put a renewed focus on child protection. He would work with LAs on the need to recruit more foster carers. He promised to report back to the House in a year's time on the progress that had been made and ended by saying:

> For every child who needs our protection – we must reform this system.
> For every family who needs our help and support – we must reform this system.
> For every child or young person in care who deserves a safe, stable and loving home – we must reform this system. This is a moral imperative, and we must all rise to the challenge.

On 21st July 2022, the Children's Social Care Implementation Board was set up and its membership announced. Currently, it is chaired by a DfE minister and includes Amanda Spielman, HMCI; Isabelle Trowler, Chief Social Worker for Children and Families in England; and Dame Rachel de Souza, England's Children's Commissioner. As well as the people not mentioned here, three board members with direct experience of the care system are due to be appointed ahead of the first full board meeting.

The next conversation is with Richard Broadhurst, an ex-social work manager whose role is now that of assistant head in a secondary special school, where his responsibilities include being the DSL, Inter-Agency Liaison, CiN, leading teams of social work students on placement in the school and offering safeguarding supervision to DSLs in other schools. Richard mentions the value of systemic working, family therapy, and family group conferences. These approaches are explained as follows:

Information point: Systemic working and family therapy

Systemic working In the 1970s, cybernetics, the study of different systems, whether for instance mechanical, electrical, physical, biological, or social systems, considered how to make sense of the world through exploring relationship patterns. This led to systemic practice being used to focus on whole family systems rather than the individuals within the family, and how change might be achieved through looking at the impact of family relationships on children.

Family therapy This, in turn, led to its practical application in the form of family therapy, which assumes that the problems that have arisen lie within the family rather than a single person within it. Family therapy is usually provided by a psychologist, clinical social worker, or a licensed therapist, who will help family members to improve the communication between them and consider their relationships and behaviour towards each other and how they can work together to resolve any conflicts that have arisen.

Family Group Conference (FGC) This is a mechanism for making sure that families and their networks are placed at the centre of the professional decisions that affect their lives such as care proceedings. Central to the approach is the belief that children are likely to have better outcomes if the immediate and extended family are involved in planning, placement, and contact decisions throughout their upbringing. FGCs are guided by a facilitator who ensures everyone is heard and their contribution is valued and that the voice of the child is central to all decision-making.

In conversation with Richard Broadhurst, ex–social worker and assistant head.

Q. What made you decide to become a social worker?

A. I was involved in youth work through my local church as a teenager. I did not know what I wanted to do when I left school and therefore did many different jobs until I was encouraged to apply for a role as a residential child care officer in a children's home. In that role I learned much about child development and how to meet the needs of children who have experienced harm and most of all how relationships with a reliable adult can be a positive vehicle for change. It was a tough job, which included the experience of a police investigation into historical allegations that a manager had abused a number of children. This process helped me to understand how vulnerable children in care needed contact with family members and professionals that was unfettered so that they could listen to and advocate for them.

The experiences of residential care led me to train to become a social worker, in 1991. I was able to work in assessment, CiN and child protection teams as a social worker and then I became a team manager – in child protection, out of hours (which included adult services, mental health and children's services) and disabled children teams. I was an independent reviewing officer for a while. I managed social work teams in various parts of the local authority, and I had excellent continuous professional development, management support, and supervision that enabled me to gain practise expertise over thousands of interactions.Each role taught me something more about how to manage services in a way that was less defensive and more responsive to need by learning how other services (children and adolescent mental health services (CAMHS), youth offending teams (YOTs). Adult Social Care, Police and Schools) worked and making good working relationships with my peers in those services. I enjoyed learning more about different aspects of child development; the challenges of families caring for children with life limiting conditions, neurological, and developmental conditions; and how to apply such approaches to supporting families, as systemic working family therapy and family group conferencing.

Q. How did you come to be on the Senior Leadership Team (SLT) of a school?

A. I retired on the grounds ill health and cared for my parents, until they died. I was then approached by a creative and inspiring school leader, Marijke Miles, head teacher of Baycroft School. She knew of my experience and asked me to undertake safeguarding training for her staff. This eventually led to me being appointed as a part-time assistant head and DSL. My experience of working in different settings has always pulled me towards schools. This is where children and their parents and carers are most familiar – rather than the offices of social care. I tried to make sure that meetings were held in school, where possible. I had several years' experience working with disabled children, their families, and carers, which I found to be a richly rewarding professional and personal experience.

Q. What is your involvement with social work students?

A. Marijke Miles encouraged me to set up a service that she and my wife Penny (a registered social worker) developed in a previous school. This model uses social work students on 70- or 100-day placements to increase the pastoral capacity significantly. Each student has an allocated caseload of children and families they work with – offering advice, guidance and assistance. In addition, they work with other agencies and services to create good joined up responses to need and risk. They do not replace the function of Child In Need or safeguarding responses but augment them. This year, I worked with eight social work students from Chichester and Portsmouth Universities. I am no longer a registered social worker, but I use my social work experience, knowledge, and skills to manage and supervise the team that we have created. School staff see the child daily and parents and carers get to know and trust them which makes offering support at school and at home effective. The work of the social work students has had a positive impact on the children, their carers, and the teaching staff.

Q. What do you see as the value of supervision?

A. Effective work with people requires that the "helper" has time to reflect on their intervention, to learn and to make sure they are responding appropriately and safely – for themselves and for the other. This reflection and thinking time is known in social work as supervision. Increasingly, staff in schools are having to respond to safeguarding or mental health issues that would have been seen as the responsibility of social care or CAMHS specialists. Even when situations have been referred and assessed by specialist services, school staff must deal with the results of the poverty, poor housing, impaired parenting capacity, unmet mental health needs, and emerging disabilities. These issues can be so overwhelming that they can overtake the ability to think and to act appropriately. Therefore, it is vital that those supporting children and families can discuss and reflect on how they feel and what to do next. That is why supervision must include problem-solving.

The need for supervision for school staff is becoming recognised by DfE, although it is not embedded in practice. KCSiE [Keeping Children Safe in Education] 2022 has not made it a requirement. However, I offer supervision, not only to the trainees and deputy DSLs in my own school, but to DSLs in other schools, including secondary schools. The feedback suggests that it is helpful.

Q. Do you think some of the recommendations in Josh MacAlister review of children's social care will help to move things forward?

A. I agree with his analysis and many of his recommendations about how to re-make children's social care. He comes up with ideas about investing in early intervention and support for families at a much earlier stage than we see at the moment. Prof Eileen Munro (2011) made the case for reform of the child protection system that would help professionals make the best judgements about helping children and families. This included a massive investment in early help that was available to all, like Sure Start, and helped professionals and family members to work together over time. This approach is described in the MacAlister Report.

He describes the "Mockingbird", model which was developed by fostering professionals and has similarities with FGC's huge flexibility to support children and young people at all stages of their journey through care. Support groups called "Constellations" might include young people in Kinship Care and Special Guardianship orders, adoptive families, children and their key workers from residential care, parent and child placements, and young people under staying put and shared lives arrangements. This is an interesting development and one which attempts to maintain connection between children in care and their family and kinship networks. However, another pressing issue that is described in the report is increasing number of referrals to social care in England; increasing number of child protection investigations (called section 47 enquiries); and there are now just over 80,000 Children in Care (Looked After Children). Demand for placements means that they are ever more expensive and far away from family and friendship networks, including the school.

According to the National Society for the Prevention of Cruelty to Children (NSPCC), the average number of children killed by their parents or carers has been much the same for several years. The reasons why this number isn't decreasing, despite almost total emphasis on safeguarding and child protection, is **the** central issue to be resolved. This can only happen if there is vast investment into all children's services – social care, schools, NHS, and local authorities. If the government wants to implement the report at no cost – I fear that the result will be cosmetic and the whole system of support, care, and protection will fail.

Q. Is there anything else you would like to add?

A. Children and families in need have a right to be helped and society has a responsibility to support them. The most effective way to reduce harm to children is to reduce poverty, poor housing, and the poor mental and physical health of parents and carers. Multi-agency responses to children in the first five years of their life and redistribution of wealth through tax credits were shown to have a made a generational difference. We should demand that government reinstates these initiatives as an investment in the future of our society.

Conclusions

Having looked at education more generally in the first chapter of this book, and then more specifically at the education of children who need additional support in Chapter 2, this chapter has concentrated on developments in children's social care. The following chapter winds up Part One of this book by looking at developments in the health service, including health's involvement in the physical and mental health of young people and their wellbeing, before focusing on how the services of education, health, and social care are moving closer together.

References

British Association of Social Workers (BASW) (2022) *Professional Capabilities Framework.* Available from https://www.basw.co.uk/social-work-training/professional-capabilities-framework-pcf

Children's Commissioner (2022) *Children's Social Care – Putting Children's Voice at the Heart of Reform.* Available from https://www.childrenscommissioner.gov.uk/report/childrens-social-care-putting

DfE (2011) The Munro Review of Child Protection: Final Report A child-centred system. Available from Munro-Review.pdf (publishing.service.gov.uk).

DfE (2018) *Improving the Educational Outcomes of Children in Need of Health and Protection, Interim Findings.* Available from https://assets.publishing.service.gov.uk/government/uploads/system/uploads/attachment_data/file/762826/Children_in_Need_of_help_and_protection-Interim_findings.pdf

DfE (2019) *Help, Protection Education: Concluding the Children in Need Review.* Available from https://assets.publishing.service.gov.uk/government/uploads/system/uploads/attachment_data/file/809236/190614_CHILDREN_IN_NEED_PUBLICATION_FINAL.pdf

DfE (2020) *Social Workers to Work with Teachers in Schools.* Available from https://www.gov.uk/government/news/social-workers-to-work-with-teachers-in-schools

DfE (2022) *Pupil Premium: Overview.* Available from https://www.gov.uk/government/publications/pupil-premium/pupil-premium

Gov.UK (1989) *Children Act.* Available from https://www.legislation.gov.uk/ukpga/1989/41/contents

Gov.UK (2003) *The Victoria Climbie Inquiry: Report of an Enquiry by Lord Laming.* Available from https://www.gov.uk/government/publications/the-victoria-climbie-inquiry-report-of-an-inquiry-by-lord-laming

Gov.UK (2004) *Children Act.* Available from https://www.legislation.gov.uk/ukpga/2004/31/contents

Gov.Uk (2008) *Children and Young Person's Act.* Available from https://www.legislation.gov.uk/ukpga/2008/23/contents

Gov.UK (2017) *Children and Social Work Act.* Available from https://www.legislation.gov. uk/ukpga/2017/16/contents/enacted

HM Government (2018) *Working Together to Safeguard Children.* Available from https:// assets.publishing.service.gov.uk/government/uploads/system/uploads/attachment_data/ file/942454/Working_together_to_safeguard_children_inter_agency_guidance.pdf

HM Treasury (2003) *Every Child Matters.* Available from https://assets.publishing.service. gov.uk/government/uploads/system/uploads/attachment_data/file/272064/5860.pdf

https://hansard.parliament.uk/lords/2022-05-24/debates/DBE7D5F5-976C-4153-B44B-0B6D9E53565C/IndependentReviewOfChildren'SSocialCare

https://educationhub.blog.gov.uk/2022/03/16/social-workers-are-without-a-doubt-unsung-heroes-and-we-must-all-strive-to-champion-and-celebrate-their-important-work/

https://childrenscommissioner.gov.uk/help-at-hand/

MacAlister, J. (2021) *The Interim Report – Independent Review of Children's Social Care.* Available from https://childrenssocialcare.independent-review.uk/wp-content/uploads/ 2022/06/IRCSC_The_Case_for_Change_27.05.22.pdf

MacAlister, J. (2022a) *Independent Review of Children's Social Care: Final Report.* Available from https://childrenssocialcare.independent-review.uk

MacAlister, J. (2022b) *Independent Review of Children's Social Care. Recommendation Annexes May 2022 Additional Detail on Review Recommendations.* Available from https://childrens socialcare.independent-review.uk/wp-content/uploads/2022/05/Recommendation-annexes.pdf

MacAlister, J. (2022c) *Independent Review of Children's Social Care. Costing and Outline CBA of the Independent Review of Children's Social Care Recommendations Modelling Assumptions Technical Note.* Available from https://childrenssocialcare.independent-review.uk/wp-content/uploads/2022/05/Costing-technical-report.pdf

National Association of Virtual Headteachers (2022) Available from https://navsh.org.uk/

4   The Health and Care Act 2022

Implementing integrated care systems

> Given the significant overlap between the education, SEND, social care systems
> and the NHS, it is vital that we grasp the opportunity of these major reforms to
> work towards a more integrated support system for children. Otherwise, this will
> be another missed opportunity to make a real difference to children's lives.
>
> (Children's Commissioner's response to *The independent review of
> children's social care*)

After focusing on the reviews of SEND and children's social care, Chapter 4
completes Part One of the book, by turning to what is happening in the health
service in terms of children and young people. Concentrating first on the development of the NHS and then on the joining up between health and social care,
the chapter moves on to illustrate two very different ways in which even broader
partnerships have a significant part to play in the lives of young people. The first
example is about keeping children safe, which has been a concern over very many
years and includes a conversation with a former police officer who is an expert in
safeguarding. The second example is about a much more recent development,
that of social prescribing and how it can be used to improve the wellbeing of
people of all ages. Ending the chapter is a conversation with a head teacher who
established his own school for pupils who needed an environment in which they
could thrive.

The History of the NHS

> The NHS may be the proudest achievement of our modern society.
>
> (Opening quote from the *Five Year Forward View*)

In 1942, a civil servant named William Beveridge, published the *Beveridge Report*
on the need for a National Health Service (NHS). This explained that free medical
services would cover access to doctors, dentists, hospitals, and maternity services. A
post-war Labour Government was determined to make these changes and to establish a welfare state. So, in 1946, the NHS Act was passed. Two years later, the NHS
was established, helping to replace the fear people had that they would be unable
to pay for the treatment they needed if they became ill, with the reassurance that

DOI: 10.4324/9781003333203-6

everyone would be entitled to free healthcare. Money from taxes was used to create a cradle-to-grave service.

Since then, an unwavering conviction that universal healthcare should remain has not changed, but the context has altered with the NHS costing more every year. In 1952, prescription charges were introduced. More recently, eye tests and dental treatment are no longer covered for everyone. In 1998, NHS Direct was launched to relieve pressure on GPs and A&E Departments. This was replaced in 2014 by NHS 111, the nurse-led telephone information service, providing basic healthcare advice and directing those with more serious conditions to the appropriate part of the wider service. Meanwhile, the private health sector has grown in parallel with the NHS.

In 2003, a Health and Social Care Act established NHS Foundation Trusts, which, in a similar way to schools becoming academies, gave them greater freedom to make their own decisions. (NHS Foundation Trusts are semi-autonomous organisational units within the National Health Service in England). In 2009, the Care Quality Commission (CQC) was established as a new regulator for primary care services, including hospitals, GP practices, dental practices, and care homes. In 2012, the Health and Social Care Act brought in a wide range of reforms, including health and wellbeing boards. These were established to bring together the NHS, public health, adult social care, and children's services, to plan how best to meet local needs and tackle inequalities in health. The same Act saw primary care trusts replaced by clinical commissioning groups (CCGs). These were run by groups of GPs and were later absorbed into integrated care services as part of the Health and Care Act 2022. Before discussing this recent piece of legislation, however, there are three key documents that explain more about the evolution of the NHS.

Key NHS documents

In addition to legislation and other changes already mentioned, three of the more recent key documents resulting in significant changes to the health service include

- The Five Year Forward View (2014)
- The Next Steps on the NHS Five Year Forward View (2017)
- The NHS Long Term Plan (2019)

Oct 2014 Five Year Forward View

The Five Year Forward View set out a vision for the future of the NHS, which included why change was needed, what it might look like, and how it might be achieved. One of the changes was to have a different relationship with patients, carers, and the general public, so that it would be more of an equal partnership rather than patients being told what to do by the professionals. It was also concerned with a shift from treatment to the importance of prevention, with patients and communities taking greater responsibility for keeping themselves healthy.

It was a hopeful sign when, in 2015, the NHS introduced sustainability and transformation plans, which served as the forerunner for bringing in integrated care systems (ICSs) across England. If these had been in place before the pandemic struck, it might have helped with the lack of joined-up planning between health and social care, which meant people remaining in hospital when they could have been discharged, if they had had a suitable package of support, either in their own homes or in a care home.

Next Steps on the NHS Five Year Forward View

Moving on to the second of the three key documents, *Next Steps on the NHS Five Year Forward View* reported on progress made in the three years since it had been published and outlined what needed to be done over the remaining two years of the plan. This included

- How to take the strain off A&E and free up hospital beds by closer working between different providers
- Increasing investment in mental health, greater access to psychological or "talking therapies", with children being able to access care locally
- Having more routes into training for frontline services
- Harnessing the potential of technology and innovation.

In an interview for an article entitled *The Journey to Integrated Care Systems* (September 2018), Sir Chris Ham, Chief Executive of The King's Fund (a charitable organisation working for over 100 years to improve health and care in England), wrote:

> The tide has turned away from competition towards collaboration, with different areas being given permission to test how to join up care for their populations. Slowly but surely, a focus on places and populations is replacing the emphasis on organisations.
>
> (2018: 11)

NHS Long Term Plan

Having come to the end of its five year plan, the NHS set out what it hoped to achieve over the next ten years. This included the aim for all areas to be involved in ICSs by April 2021. To enable this to happen, improved funding had been secured for the next five years. The first chapter talks of patients having more control over their lives and benefitting from better joining up between services in their area. The third chapter promises a greater focus on children's health and on learning disability and autism in people of all ages. As a result, a Children and Young People Transformation Programme was established, with the work being overseen by a Children and Young People Transformation Programme Board, bringing together partners across health, care, and education. Its membership includes six youth board members to ensure the voices of children and young people are represented in decision-making.

The lead up to the Health and Care Act 2022

After putting forward recommendations about what should be in an NHS Bill, the NHS followed this up by producing recommendations on legislating for ICSs, to ensure they were put on a statutory footing. This was followed by the Department of Health and Social Care (DHSC) presenting its White Paper: *Integration and innovation: working together to improve health and social care for all*. In the fore-word, the government refers to the influence the pandemic had on what needed to change:

> This paper sets out our legislative proposals for a Health and Care Bill. It aims to build on the incredible collaborations we have seen through COVID and shape a system that's better able to serve people in a fast-changing world.

Shortly before the Bill itself was published, and being all too aware that it looked as if the Bill would ignore the existence of children and young people, a letter was sent to Sajid Javid, at that time secretary of state at the DHSC, from the Young People's Health Policy Influencing Group (HPIG). Hosted by the Council for Disabled Children (CDC), HPIG acts as a voice for babies, children, and young people's physical and mental health issues in England. The letter refers to the gov-ernment's goal of improving population health, tackling health inequalities, and preventing poor health later in life, pointing out that this could not be achieved without a strong focus on children and young people:

> However, we have serious concerns that these proposed changes have not been planned with children and young people in mind. By failing to recognise that children and young people are a distinct population who use a distinct health and care system with its own workforce, legislation and integration challenges, the reforms will not achieve the long-term improvement to health outcomes you intend.
>
> (letter written 14.05.21)

Health and Care Bill 2021

In July 2021 the Health and Care Bill began its passage through Parliament. Its purpose was said to be to establish a legislative framework that supports collabora-tion rather than competition. This has an interesting echo with changes to the education system, where there has also been a shift from stressing competition to talking about the need for schools to work in partnership with each other. While the Bill contained new powers for the secretary of state over the health and care system, the most significant change related to the integrated care boards (ICBs) that were due to replace CCGs across the country from 1 July 2022.

Information point: Integrated Care Systems (ICSs)

In 2015, the NHS introduced Sustainability and Transformation Plans (STPs), which served as the forerunner for bringing in Integrated Care Systems (ICSs) across England.

The purpose of ICSs is to bring together NHS organisations, LAs. and others in a practical way to deliver the "triple integration" of:

1)   primary and specialist care
2)   physical and mental health services
3)   health with social care.

Each ICS has:

•   An Integrated Care Board (ICB) responsible for NHS strategic planning and allocation decisions
•   An Integrated Care Partnership (ICP) responsible for bringing together a wider set of partners to develop a plan to address the broader health and social care needs of the local population.

All ICBs are required to address the needs of those aged 0–25 in their forward plans, due to amendments to the Bill.

Amendments to the Health and Care Bill

After months of HPIG working with civil servants and parliamentarians on wording the amendments, in March 2022, these were debated in the House of Lords, resulting in babies and young people up to the age of 25 being included on the face of the Bill. The specific commitments in relation to ICSs were that ICBs would be required to set out the steps it will take to address the needs of babies and young people in its forward plan. In addition, NHS England has to issue statutory guidance which will include a statement that each ICB must nominate an executive children's lead, ensuring leadership for babies and young people on every ICB.

A further amendment was about improving the sharing of information across all children sector organisations. The government acknowledged the serious challenges with sharing relevant information about children, while recognising the benefits of a single identifier that would bring together disparate records. To address this, an amendment was made to the Act requiring the government to lay a report before Parliament within a year, setting out the government's policy on a consistent identifier for children and how it might be achieved across health, children's social care, the police, and education settings.

Policy paper by DHSC and DLUHC

Shortly before the Health and Social Care Bill became an Act, a Policy Paper was issued jointly by the DHSC and the Department for Levelling Up, Housing and Communities (DLUHC). In their joint forward, Michael Gove and Sajid Javid wrote:

> The storms we have weathered over the past 2 years have been a great test, but also a great teacher. ... So, as we recover and level up, it is right that we draw on our experience of the pandemic to bridge the gaps between health and social care.
>
> (Paragraph 1.14)

The paper ends by talking about the support the government will give to promote the benefits of flexibility and local learning, while stating that this agenda is more likely to be realised by local organisations than through central prescription.

Health and Social Care Act 2022

In April 2022, the Health and Care Bill became an Act. This was around the same time as the publication of the Schools White Paper; the SEND Green Paper; and the publication of the review of children's social care. All these major policy changes affect children, young people, and their families, and all rely on strong multi-agency working. Linking these pieces of policy together will take a great deal of work at both national and local level.

The Health and Care Act established the two-part statutory ICSs, with an Integrated Care Board (ICB) and an Integrated Care Partnership (ICP). A key premise is that much of the activity will be driven by commissioners and providers collaborating over smaller geographies within ICSs, often referred to as places, and through teams delivering services working together on even smaller footprints, usually referred to as neighbourhoods. While the Health and Social Care Act 2012 sought to strengthen the role of competition within the health system, NHS organisations were now being told to collaborate rather than compete, in order to respond to the challenges facing their local services. This new approach is sometimes referred to as place-based planning.

Timeline: The evolution of the NHS

1942	The **Beveridge Report** confirmed the need for a National Health Service
1946	NHS Act passed and established two years later
1952	Prescription charges introduced
1998	NHS Direct launched; replaced in 2014 by NHS 111
2002	District health authorities replaced by strategic health authorities and primary care trusts
2003	The Health and Social Care Act leads to establishment of NHS foundation trusts
2009	Care Quality Commission created as a regulator for health and social care services

2012	The Health and Social Care Act replaces strategic health authorities and primary care trusts with NHS England
2014	NHS sets out changes in *The Five Year Forward View*
2015	NHS sustainability and transformation plans brought in and were a forerunner of integrated care systems
2016	Sustainability and transformation plans help join up local services
2017	*Next Steps on the NHS Five Year Forward View*
2019	**NHS Long Term Plan** sets the direction for the next ten years.
2021	White Paper: *Integration and innovation: working together to improve health and social care for all*
2022	The Health and Care Act

The NHS moving forward

The NHS has been caught up in a constantly changing world of greater expectations in terms of a more personalised and accessible service, while at the same time trying to keep pace with the cost of improved technology, ever more expensive drugs and treatments, and the need for more qualified staff. As with other services, there have been ongoing concerns about workload and training enough staff to keep up with demand.

Training and employment opportunities

In a similar way to other professions, more flexible routes into training are becoming established. The list that follows will apply differently depending on the job being sought, but includes:

- Apprenticeships
- Nursing associates
- Online qualifications
- "Earn and learn" support

Some of these are backed by a new post-qualification employment guarantee.

The largest employer in the UK healthcare sector is the NHS, which employs more than 1.5 million people in 350 different roles. Some include working across education and health, or health and social care. As well as the NHS, there are opportunities to work in private healthcare or in voluntary and non-profit organisations. Places of work may be as varied as hospitals and clinics; schools, colleges and universities; residential and non-residential care organisations; and private or independent organisations. Whether the work is in the health service; children's social care; or in pre-school, school, or FE settings, a major concern is always about safeguarding. The next section is about keeping children safe, which has been an ongoing concern for very many years.

Safeguarding

There is sometimes a tendency to use the words safeguarding and child protection interchangeably. Although they are interrelated, they do not have the same meaning, as child protection is part of the safeguarding process.

<u>Safeguarding</u> This relates to the action taken to promote the welfare of children and to protect them from harm. It involves protecting them from abuse, preventing their health or development being harmed, and ensuring children are kept safe and cared for as they grow up.

<u>Child protection</u> This is about the process of safeguarding children. The focus is on trying to identify and protect children who are suffering, or who are likely to suffer, significant harm.

The UK's four nations have their own safeguarding and child protection laws. Each nation is responsible for its own policies and laws around education, health, and social welfare. Although the child protection systems are different in each nation, they are based on similar principles. In England, the Local Authority Designated Officer (LADO) works within Children's Services and gives advice and guidance to employers, organisations, and other individuals if they raise concerns about the behaviour of an adult who is working with children and young people. LADOs ensure that there is a robust response to any concerns raised about professionals.

The first Working Together guidance was published by the government in 1989. This was revised in 2006, following Lord Laming's inquiry into the death of Victoria Climbie which was mentioned in the opening chapter of this book. There have been other revisions since, partly to reflect changes in legislation, but the 2018 guidance is the one that is currently still in use. A brief update in 2022, for instance, reflected the change from CCGs to ICBs, as well as the change from Public Health England (PHE) to the Office for Health Improvement and Disparities (OHID).

To give it its full title, ***Working Together to Safeguard Children – A guide to inter-agency working to safeguard and promote the welfare of children*** refers to the statutory duty placed on the three key agencies: the LA, the police, and the CCG – now replaced by the ICB. However, as it says in the introduction, everyone who comes into contact with children and families has a role to play. The guidance defines safeguarding as:

- Protecting children from maltreatment
- Preventing impairment of children's mental and physical health or development
- Ensuring that children can grow up in circumstances consistent with the provision of safe and effective care
- Taking action to enable all children to have the best outcomes.

It goes on to specify that it applies in its entirety to all schools and to all children up to the age of 18:

> Schools, colleges and other educational settings must also have regard to statutory guidance "Keeping Children Safe in Education", which provides further guidance as to how they should fulfil their duties in respect of safeguarding and promoting the welfare of children in their care.

> (2018: 62)

The reference to ***Keeping children safe in education – Statutory guidance for schools and colleges*** (known as KCSiE), is a reminder of the need for those in educational settings to read and follow both sets of guidance, which are updated regularly. Among the changes which took effect from September 2022, the term peer-on-peer abuse has been replaced by child-on-child abuse, in order to clarify that the focus of the document is on children and not on adults. The latest version has also been altered to include 16–19 academies and FE colleges. Staff and governors are required to confirm in writing that they have read Part One. Ofsted inspects safeguarding processes very thoroughly, by seeing how the single central record is maintained; checking the training staff and governors have undertaken, including safer recruitment; and interviewing those primarily responsible for the strategic overview of safeguarding in the school or college.

As mentioned in the previous chapter of this book, in the final report of his review into children's social care, Josh MacAlister put forward a number of recommendations for strengthening safeguarding, with everyone being clearer about their roles and responsibilities. Recommendation 13 in chapter 8 of MacAlister's review asks for schools to be made one of the statutory safeguarding partners.

To end this section on safeguarding, there is a conversation with Chris Miller, a former senior police officer with substantial experience of safeguarding. Since retiring from the police force, he has undertaken many roles, including his present one as chair of Harrow's Safeguarding Adults Board and chair and independent scrutineer of the Harrow Safeguarding Children Partnership.

In conversation with Chris Miller, former senior police officer and expert on safeguarding issues

Q. You have a significant lead role for safeguarding in your area – how were you appointed?

A. I was appointed in 2017 following a public advert and a series of interviews conducted by the safeguarding partners in Harrow: the LA, the police and the clinical commissioning group (CCG) now known as the integrated care board (ICB). In my previous role as a senior police officer, I had a significant safeguarding role, and had worked for a charity who supported victims of domestic abuse. Prior to my appointment with Harrow, I held a similar position in Barnet as safeguarding lead.

Q. What relationship does your role have with education, health, and social care?

A. In relation to Harrow Safeguarding Adults Board (HSAB), and the Harrow Safeguarding Children Partnership (HSCP), both the LA and the local Integrated Care Board (ICB) – which is the organising and commissioning arm of the NHS – are statutory members, the third being the police. Legally, the HSCP is their partnership and they invite (they can even compel) other bodies to take part in the arrangements. In Harrow, as in the rest of the UK, schools and colleges have been invited to be and are members.

The problem with the question lies in the word "education". This isn't a meaningful term in a legal sense. Whereas locally there is one police force, one ICB, and one LA, there is a myriad of schools, colleges, and nurseries, each of which is a separate legal entity. Notwithstanding this difficulty, in Harrow we have two head teachers (one primary, one secondary) and a college principal on a coordinating executive body (the Harrow Strategic Safeguarding Partnership) which oversees the work both of the HSAB and the HSCP. We also have sitting on the HSCP itself a number of head teachers who represent primary, secondary, special, private, and early years education, as well as a college representative.

Q. What are the formal partnerships between education, health, and social care in terms of safeguarding?

A. The HSAB and the Health and Wellbeing Board (HWB) are both statutory bodies, but they don't have representation from education. The HWB is a partnership between the ICB, Primary Care (GPs, pharmacies, and so on) and the LA (social care and public health). It oversees the commissioning of some health and social care resources and the prioritisation of certain public health initiatives. The HSCP is a statutory partnership and has good representation from schools and Early Years, while the Strategic Safeguarding Partnership is non-statutory, but is Harrow's attempt to have senior coordinating oversight.

Both the ICB and the LA have some discretionary spend and the HWB oversees and coordinates that spend. It can also hold to account NHS providers for their delivery of certain nationally required programmes (eg vaccination programmes). There is also the Child Death Overview Panel, which is another statutory body examining child deaths in the area, in this case in NW London. Most child deaths occur in children under one and so education in the form of individual schools is involved as necessary, which is not that common. School age child deaths are mercifully rare.

Q. How are these partnerships funded?

A. There are a couple of issues here. The coordination of these partnerships is a back-office function, which is relatively light spend. Then there is the delivery of the partnership programmes, which can involve considerable spend. The back-office funding (the coordination of agendas, arrangement of papers, analysis of results) is funded by the statutory partners, not necessarily on an equitable footing. The delivery of partnership programmes comes out of each organisation's local budgets and depends on the appetite of each partner for using their discretionary spend on partnership initiatives. For instance, a multi-agency criminal justice diversion programme for adolescents involving the police, social care, CAMHS, and schools would be funded according to the aspiration and vision of each of the contributing agencies. Such initiatives are often highly personality driven, depend on determined and focused leadership, and sometimes die away when the leader leaves. Sometimes there is central government funding for initiatives. Too often, when the funding dries up, the initiative stops.

Q. How have the relationships between education, health, and social care in terms of safeguarding changed over the last 10 or 20 years?

A. The concept of safeguarding had its origins in the Laming report into the death of Victoria Climbie. That inquiry found that there were significant gaps in knowledge, intelligence, and action between and among the various agencies that could have protected her. That led to the Children Act of 2004, which in 2006 led to the establishment of Safeguarding Boards. These are local partnerships of statutory agencies whose work brought them into contact with children. It also led to Working Together, the guidance to be followed by agencies in bringing about effective local delivery.

The thrust of the Children Act was very much part of a pattern of the development of shared agendas. In 1998 the Crime and Disorder Act had imposed similar joint working requirements on police, LA and Health in relation to crime and disorder. So, whether keeping people safe on the streets or children safe at home, the same philosophy applies; namely, that a shared vision, pooled information, and joint goals would lead to better outcomes than operating in isolation. The difficulty with the outworking of this approach is that central government did not and does not always model the behaviour that they expect of local partners. So, the police, the LA and Health are assessed differently and rarely is the effectiveness of a local partnership commented on in inspections.

The driver for integration has been through statutory avenues, which often have a review at their origin: Climbie review → Children Act → Safeguarding Boards. But the relationship between the partners has been transformed over the past 20 years. Senior leaders in these bodies all have a history of working with others. However, while partnerships now have a resilient steady state about them, it still takes major events to move things on. Most public sector leaders are very cautious and still quite insular. That is probably related to the governance of local delivery. Police report to a distant mayor; LAs report to politicians, who are short-term and local; and Health is in a constant state of flux and reorganisation and is always short of cash.

Q. A recommendation in Josh MacAlister's Review suggested that schools should be made a statutory safeguarding partner. How would this work and do you think it would make a difference?

A. The report suggests that one option for delivering this would be that, within a given area, schools nominate one representative with the seniority to work alongside the LA's chief executive, the accountable officer for a CCG (soon-to-be ICB), and a chief officer of police, to take a shared and equal responsibility for safeguarding arrangements. This would require a mechanism to enable this representative to come to meetings able to make decisions on behalf of schools within an area. I would just add that the three statutory partners all have budget and resources to move around to back up partnership agreements. I'm not sure that a school's rep could move any budget or resource (probably not their own and definitely not anyone else's), so, in that sense, the rep might not really be an equal partner.

The review believes it is likely that representatives would need to be at the level of the CEO of a multi-academy trust (MAT). The upcoming reforms to the schools system, whereby all schools might become part of MATs, means that this may become a viable option. These reforms include a new collaborative standard, which will require trusts to work constructively with each other, their LAs and wider public services. This could be invoked to bring the local schools' systems together to participate collectively in arrangements. Better alternative models may be available, but in any event, the safeguarding arrangements will need to establish the means for all schools to take full responsibility for their role in safeguarding and promoting the welfare of children.

The conversation with Chris illustrates not only the vital nature of safeguarding and child protection, but the extent to which it depends on having clear procedures in place and the willingness of everyone involved to share information across professional boundaries. Throughout this book, the need for professionals to work together has been emphasised and this is an area where it can make a critical difference to the lives of children and young people. While safeguarding and child protection are very clear examples of the need for different services to pool information and many agencies are involved in this critical work, an even greater number of people are involved in social prescribing. In fact, some forms of social prescribing can bring whole communities together.

Social prescribing

Social prescribing is sometimes referred to as community referral. It is a means of enabling GPs, nurses, and other health and care professionals to refer people of all ages, including children, to a range of local, non-clinical services. Such an approach seeks to address people's needs in a more holistic manner and to support individuals in taking greater control of their own health. In January 2022, the Office for Health Improvement and Disparities (OHID), formerly known as Public Health England, issued updated guidance, setting out the core principles of this holistic approach to addressing individual needs, which moves away from seeing medication as the only prescription. Although it is initiated by health, it includes partnerships from across the services and beyond.

Social prescribing schemes can involve a variety of activities which are typically provided by voluntary and community sector organisations. Some examples include:

- Volunteering and other work in the community
- Arts activities
- Group learning
- Gardening
- Befriending
- Cookery and healthy eating advice
- Sporting activities

Link workers

Social prescribing enables all local agencies to refer people to a link worker. Link workers give individuals time to focus on how to improve their lives. They can connect people of all ages to community groups and agencies for practical and emotional support. Referrals to link workers can come from a wide range of local agencies, including:

- general practice
- local authorities
- pharmacies
- multi-disciplinary teams
- hospital discharge teams
- allied health professionals
- fire service
- police
- job centres
- social care services
- housing associations and voluntary, community, and social enterprise organisations.

Self-referrals are also encouraged. The National Academy for Social Prescribing says its work is:

> to create partnerships, across the arts, health, sports, leisure, and the natural environment, alongside other aspects of our lives, to promote health and wellbeing at a national and local level. We will champion social prescribing and the work of local communities in connecting people for wellbeing.

Social prescribing for children

Although NHS England's Long Term Plan pledged 1,000 new social prescribing link workers by 2020/21 and at least 900,000 people accessing social prescribing services by 2023/24, there was no specific mention of this covering children and young people. However, the idea that social prescribing can benefit people of all ages is beginning to gather momentum. In 2021, the National Children's Bureau (NCB) produced *Social prescribing for children and young people*. This lists the following as ways in which children's wellbeing and confidence are enhanced through this approach:

- Helping them to meet other young people
- Sparking motivation through a new interest
- Being more active
- Feeling more connected and less isolated.

Interestingly, these tally very closely with the NHS's Five Steps to Wellbeing mentioned at the start of this book. A study the NCB made into social prescribing for young people showed that it did indeed increase their confidence and wellbeing. Currently, as part of the government's wider rollout of green social prescribing (GSP), Preventing and Tackling Mental Ill Health through Green Social Prescribing Project is underway.

This chapter ends with a conversation with David Duncan, who founded his own school and ran it for 30 years. Before he retired, the school became part of Aspris Children's Services (formerly known as Priory Education), which is a private company running special schools and colleges, children's homes, and fostering services. The conversation with David is followed by three case studies of pupils who were at the school when he was the head teacher.

In conversation with David Duncan

Q. What made you decide to make teaching your career?

A. When I was a pupil, I was seriously injured playing rugby and I was told I must give up contact sports. I didn't see why I should be put on the scrapheap because of this, so I asked the PE teacher about where I could train to teach PE. I chose Carnegie, Leeds. It was difficult getting a place but I was determined to succeed. After that, I started my teaching career at a direct grant grammar school which had weekly boarding provision. To increase my salary, I became a housemaster as well.

Q. What drew you into special education?

A. My parents had been joint houseparents of a school when I was growing up. At one stage, I stayed with a friend of the family who ran what was then described as a school for maladjusted pupils and I gained experience by helping them. Although the school was in Cumbria, most of the pupils came from Greater Manchester and Lancashire, which meant they were too far away for their families to be involved in their education. When they finished school and went home, they were out of touch with their local community. After three years at the grammar school, I was invited to go back to the school where my parents had worked, which I did.

Q. How did you come to set up your own school?

A. Knowing the difficulties of pupils being hundreds of miles from home, and being familiar with the number of pupils Lancashire were sending out of the county, I spent a year trotting back and forth every weekend between Cumbria and Lancashire to find somewhere I might start a school which would be accessible to pupils from Greater Manchester and Lancs. Having studied geography, I knew how important modality is, so I looked for where there were good road connections between the main conurbations. This would mean that families could be involved in their children's education and we could work with them as well as their children. When a farm in Rossendale came up for sale, this met all the requirements. I knew I would be able to recruit staff as well as pupils, as they could live locally and would come because the nature of the job appealed to them. The school opened in 1989.

Q. Did you always offer residential provision and what form did it take?

A. Initially, we used part of the farmhouse to accommodate those who needed to board, but I knew the kids needed to live in the community. So when I had enough funds, I recruited a teacher I knew who'd been assessed as a foster carer and installed him in a house in the local town. I'd worked in 52-week-a-year provision before and I didn't want this, because of the importance of family links and helping the family to gain a better understanding of their child. So I registered with social services for weekly boarding. I was one of the first to be registered under the 1989 Children Act and I was involved in piloting the National Standards. Later, I was able to purchase a second house. From the start, each child had their own bedroom and later, we were able to make all rooms ensuite.

When we needed more space, I rented what had originally been a pub but had been turned into four flats, each with two bedrooms, so a further eight pupils could be accommodated. Renting wasn't ideal, as you could be thrown out with six months' notice and we weren't able to make any changes. However, they proved to be a good way of introducing older pupils to getting ready for independent living.

Q. How was it that you were able to be recognised as providing a CAMHS service?

A. The in-hospital CAMHS provision was outsourced by Stockport who put it out for tender, so we put in a bid, registered it with Ofsted and the DfE, and my wife, Liz, ran the educational provision. She spent some time persuading the clinicians that the young people would benefit from a robust education programme to help prepare them for returning to mainstream education on discharge. Surprisingly, none of them had EHC plans which could have been initiated by the clinicians, but they were unaware how to do this.

Q. Did you see much change in the pupil population while you were running the school?

A. What has changed is our understanding of needs children may have which were hidden and not recognised. For instance, children with autism or mental health problems used to be put in EBD [Emotional and Behavioural Difficulties] schools, where they were terrified by the more delinquent pupils. It's much better now that there is more appropriate provision for them even if there's not enough. A paediatrician told me that the last 15 years have seen massive changes in our understanding, including children being diagnosed with both autism and ADHD.

At one stage, when David Blunkett was secretary of state for education, he asked me what made my school more successful than similar schools elsewhere. I pointed out that, as an independent school, I had some say over who comes to the school. I think of it as being like the recycling banks at the supermarket, where there are places for green, brown, and white bottles as well as paper and cardboard. It works because the waste is separated out. EBD schools were expected to take in whoever is sent to them, but I could take in those discarded by their previous schools and make them into people who can make a contribution to society. When I had a knee problem, I went to a specialist who did knees; he didn't even do hips! If we want better outcome for SEND pupils, we need a similar approach and not just what will be the cheapest way either.

Q. What made you join Aspris Services Group and what were the advantages and disadvantages?

A. I knew it wouldn't be long until Liz, my wife, and I would be ready to retire and I wanted to make the school's future more secure. I continued as head so that I could make sure the school didn't change radically by becoming part of a larger organisation. In a way, it was similar to joining a multi-academy trust. One of the main advantages was being able to have supervision through Aspris's network of hospitals and clinicians. Supervision is really important. Apart from staff being able to unload after dealing with pupils' problems, it makes them feel valued. If staff are treated well, they will give you loyalty.

Q. What do you think can help the services to work more closely together?

A. It's a question of understanding the different cultures, and, where appropriate, bringing them into a school setting. Providing education within a CAMHS service was a challenge because it was a healthcare environment. Social workers who are attached to schools develop a different perspective and it also results in families seeing the social workers in a different light. If you're supporting families where no one is used to having a job, or where there's a an idea it's not breaking the law that's wrong but getting caught, changing that kind of culture is easier to do if everyone works together.

Q. Is there anything else you'd like to say?

A. There should be an expectation that supervision is also necessary in a school setting, as it is for staff in other professions. We need to get back to evolution not revolution, to encourage kids rather than punish them. We should deal with staff in a similar way and show a degree of care and compassion.

3 Individual case studies

PJ arrived at the school in Year 10, having dropped out of high school in Year 8. During the time he was at home, he hardly left his bedroom but was obsessed with a computer game, where he'd reached the top 100 players in

Europe and wanted to be in the top ten. The upshot was he spent 18–20 hours a day playing the game; his hair became shoulder length; he didn't shower; and his father brought him food on a tray. He was brought to my school by the police after he'd assaulted his mother when she interrupted a game and he lost! I thought the only chance was to have him as a boarder.

We started to wean him off the computer and to get him to shower, brush his teeth, and join others at the meal table. Although he'd missed so much school, he was taught with his peers as, although difficult to engage in learning, he was clearly very bright. I talked to him about his interests and it transpired that he was interested in medicine, so I arranged for a surgeon friend of mine to show him round the local hospital and he was hooked.

We kept him for an extra year, by which time he'd collected nine GCSEs and we continued to support him while he moved on to a sixth form college to gain A levels in maths, chemistry, and biology. He was accepted at Manchester University to read medicine and he started well, but he had a bit of a breakdown. We supported him to work in an old people's home to regain perspective and he went back to university and completed his degree. He'd had quite a battle but with a hearty shove combined with lots of support he made it to graduation day.

YM came to us in Year 6. He had little contact with his father who lived in America. He lived with his mum, but was also heavily dependent on his maternal grandmother. When he came to us, he was rather spoilt and over-protected. There were lots of battles in trying to make him more independent and also less aggressive if he couldn't get his own way. Sometimes his violence meant physical intervention was needed.

On one occasion, I was unable to calm him down and I ended up holding him. He was incandescent with rage and had a nose bleed which meant my suit trousers had to be dry cleaned! His mum disagreed with what we had done as she thought he should be allowed to be angry and wanted to remove him from the school. Finally she saw sense and let him stay. Towards the end of Year 9, he no longer needed holding and he began to throw himself into being as good as he could be academically.

Although he was extremely upset when his grandmother died, we supported the family and he managed to achieve nine GCSEs with very good grades. We supported him through college where he got three As at A level and went on to York University to study engineering. He did so well that he stayed on to do a Master's. His mum was so proud of him that she presented the school with a trophy which is awarded annually to a student who has demonstrated outstanding academic excellence.

AB had been out of school for many years. Academically, he had been fine, but he was unable to cope with a school environment that was full of social uncertainties and unpredictability. He lacked both confidence and social skills. In the end, he refused to speak to anyone and then to attend school.

AB started school with us a on a gradual basis. We arranged for him to enter classes first and to have his usual seat before the other pupils entered. At first, he ate separately and he spent breaktimes in the library as he loved reading. As he enjoyed learning and didn't find it stressful, he was entered a year early for his GCSEs. AB wanted to study five A levels as he said he'd found GCSEs very easy. We agreed to let him do this as long as he learnt to cope with social interaction to get ready for university. We gave him tasks such as instructing younger pupils in science and going to a local shop to buy his food for lunch. He gained all five A levels with top grades.

AB has learnt to function in the local community when there is a reason for doing so. AB understands that there are times when socialising is a "necessity". He joined everyone at Christmas dinner and the Christmas quiz, speaking out in front of others to help his team. AB has completed his first year at Newcastle University as a happy, engaged, and motivated student.

It was the understanding and individualised approach they received that enabled David's former pupils to succeed when their futures might have turned out very differently.

Conclusions

The NHS has evolved and improved dramatically over the years. Patients' needs are changing, too. New treatment options are emerging and there are particular challenges in areas such as mental health, which was a concern well before the pandemic struck.

The chapters making up Part One of this book have set the scene in terms of developments across education, health and social care. Part Two is more about how interagency working is happening on the ground. A number of examples, case studies, and conversations with people working across the services are provided. The voices of young people and their parents continue to be used to bring these to life. Both parts of the book draw out some of the main threads running throughout, including the similarities in the way the services have developed and the issues they face.

References

Care Quality Commission (2009) Available from https://www.cqc.org.uk/guidance-providers/regulations-enforcement/regulations-covered-guidance

Council for Disabled Children (2021) *Social Prescribing for Children and Young People. Headstart.* Available from https://councilfordisabledchildren.org.uk/sites/default/files/uploads/attachments/Headstart%20report%20social%20prescribing_0.pdf

DHSC (2019) *National Academy for Social Prescribing.* Available from https://www.gov.uk/government/news/social-prescribing-new-national-academy-set-up

DHSC (2021) *White Paper: Integration and Innovation: Working Together to Improve Health and Social Care for All.* Available from https://www.gov.uk/government/publications/working-together-to-improve-health-and-social-care-for-all/integration-and-innovation-working-together-to-improve-health-and-social-care-for-all-html-version

Gov.Uk (1946) *NHS Act.* Available from https://www.parliament.uk/about/living-heritage/transformingsociety/livinglearning/coll-9-health1/health-01/

Gov.UK (1989) *Children Act.* Available from https://www.legislation.gov.uk/ukpga/1989/41/contents

Gov.UK (2003a) *Health and Social Care Act.* Available from https://www.legislation.gov.uk/ukpga/2003/43/contents

Gov.UK (2003b) *The Victoria Climbie Inquiry: Report of an Enquiry by Lord Laming.* Available from https://www.gov.uk/government/publications/the-victoria-climbie-inquiry-report-of-an-inquiry-by-lord-laming

Gov.UK (2012) *Health and Social Care Act.* Available from https://www.legislation.gov.uk/ukpga/2012/7/contents/enacted

Gov.Uk (2018) *Working Together to Safeguard Children a Guide to Inter-agency Working to Safeguard and Promote the Welfare of Children.* Available from https://www.gov.uk/government/publications/working-together-to-safeguard-children--2

Gov.Uk (2021) *Health and Social Care Bill.* Available from https://www.gov.uk/government/publications/health-and-care-bill-factsheets/health-and-care-bill-information

Gov.UK (2022a) *Health and Social Care Act.* Available from https://www.legislation.gov.uk/ukpga/2022/31/introduction/enacted

Gov.UK (2022b) *Keeping Children Safe in Education. Statutory Guidance for Schools and Colleges on Safeguarding Children and Safer Recruitment.* Available from https://www.gov.uk/government/publications/keeping-children-safe-in-education--2

Gov.UK (2022c) *Policy Paper – Levelling Up the United Kingdom.* Available from https://www.gov.uk/government/publications/levelling-up-the-united-kingdom

Gov.UK (2022d) *SEND Review: Right Support, Right Place, Right Time.* Available from https://assets.publishing.service.gov.uk/government/uploads/system/uploads/attachment_data/file/1063620/SEND_review_right_support_right_place_right_time_accessible.pdf

Gov.UK (2022e) *Social Prescribing: Applying All Our Health.* Available from https://www.gov.uk/government/publications/social-prescribing-applying-all-our-health

Kings Fund (2018) Ham, Sir C., *The Journey to Integrated Care Systems.* Available from https://www.kingsfund.org.uk/publications/making-sense-integrated-care-systems

MacAlister, J. (2021) *The Interim Report – Independent Review of Children's Social Care.* Available from https://childrenssocialcare.independent-review.uk/wp-content/uploads/2022/06/IRCSC_The_Case_for_Change_27.05.22.pdf

MacAlister, J. (2022) *Independent Review of Children's Social Care: Final Report.* Available from https://childrenssocialcare.independent-review.uk

National Academy for Social Prescribing (2021) *The Cross-Governmental Green Social Prescribing Project.* Available from https://www.england.nhs.uk/personalisedcare/social-prescribing/green-social-prescribing/

NCB (2021) *Letter to Sajid Javid from Young People's Health Policy Influencing Group* Available from https://www.ncb.org.uk/about-us/media-centre/news-opinion/childrens-organisations-call-urgent-updates-health-and-care-bill

NHS (2014) *Five Year Forward View*. Available from https://www.england.nhs.uk/wp-content/uploads/2014/10/5yfv-web.pdf

NHS (2015) *Sustainability and Transformation Plans*. Available from https://www.kingsfund.org.uk/publications/stps-in-the-nhs

NHS (2017) *Next Steps on the NHS Five Year Forward View*. Available from https://www.england.nhs.uk/wp-content/uploads/2017/03/NEXT-STEPS-ON-THE-NHS-FIVE-YEAR-FORWARD-VIEW.pdf

NHS (2019a) *NHS Long Term Plan*. Available from https://www.longtermplan.nhs.uk

NHS (2019b) *The NHS's Recommendations to Government and Parliament for an NHS Bill*. Available from https://www.england.nhs.uk/wp-content/uploads/2019/09/BM1917-NHS-recommendations-Government-Parliament-for-an-NHS-Bill.pdf

NHS (2021) *Legislating for Integrated Care Systems: Five Recommendations to Government and Parliament*. Available from https://www.england.nhs.uk/publication/legislating-for-integrated-care-systems-five-recommendations-to-government-and-parliament/

NHS (2022) *Children and Young People Transformation Programme – Integration of Services for Children and Young People*. Available from https://www.england.nhs.uk/get-involved/cyp/

Office for Health Improvement and Disparities (2022) *Social Prescribing: Applying All Our Health*. Available from https://www.gov.uk/government/publications/social-prescribing-applying-all-our-health/social-prescribing-applying-all-our-health

The Children's Commissioners Office (2022) *The Children's Commissioner Responds to the Independent Review of Children's Social Care*. Available from https://www.childrens commissioner.gov.uk/2022/05/23/the-childrens-commissioner-responds-to-the-independent-review-of-childrens-social-care//

UK Parliament (1942) *Beveridge Report*. Available from https://www.parliament.uk/about/living-heritage/transformingsociety/livinglearning/coll-9-health1/coll-9-health/

Part II

Establishing a successful system

5 Meeting the needs of the majority

> If mainstream provision is to meet a wide range of additional needs, it is important that schools, colleges, and settings have access to high-quality specialist support. … This typically involves specialist teachers with expertise in supporting pupils with complex needs, educational psychology, and health services such as therapy and mental health services as well as colleagues in social care services.
>
> (DfE 2022: 19)

Part One of this book focused on how education, health, and social care services are moving closer together, as emphasised by key policy documents being published at much the same time during the summer of 2022. The first two chapters of Part Two provide plenty of practical illustrations showing how schools and services are working together to improve the lives of children and young people who need additional support. At the same time, attention is paid to some of the themes that have emerged already. In this chapter, the emphasis is on increasing school attendance, improving pupil behaviour, and reducing the number of children who are excluded. There are strong connections between these three themes, which, along with interagency working, are illustrated by the conversations and case studies to follow. These are with a primary head teacher, a support services manager, an SEN Expert involved in exclusion panels, and the strategic leader of an alternative provision (AP).

Attendance

The Schools White Paper, *Opportunity for all: strong schools with great teachers for your child*, which was discussed in Chapter 1 of this book, has a chapter on 'Delivering high standards of curriculum, behaviour and attendance'. Two months after it was published, the Department for Education (DfE) brought out, 'Working together to improve school attendance'. This outlines the duties on parents, schools, and local authorities (LAs). School attendance had been an issue since before the pandemic, which interrupted the normal routine of going to school, and has become even more of an issue since. The guidance points out that regular attendance, as well as helping pupils to do well at school, is an additional safeguard for pupils who may be vulnerable. The role of the virtual school head is mentioned

DOI: 10.4324/9781003333203-8

in this context, as well as the need to be aware of any pupils with a social worker whose attendance is less than satisfactory. The DfE sets 90% attendance as the minimum level that is acceptable. At the start of the autumn term 2022, the DfE launched a three-year 1-2-1 attendance mentoring pilot, with the aim of tackling what leads to pupils not going to school regularly, such as bullying or having mental health issues. Launched in Middlesbrough, it is planned to provide tailored support to over 1,600 persistent non-attenders before expanding to other areas. All LAs are expected to have school attendance support teams, although what they are called may vary. Some LAs, for instance, have behaviour and attendance support services, so that if there are underlying behavioural issues causing pupils to be irregular attenders, these can be addressed.

Behaviour

As well as behaviour and attendance sometimes being linked together, early in 2022 the DfE launched a consultation covering both the **Revised Behaviour in Schools Guidance and Suspension and Permanent Exclusion Guidance**. This ran from the beginning of February to the end of March and resulted in the publication of two separate guidance documents. In September 2022, **Behaviour in schools – Advice for headteachers and school staff** was published, giving guidance on what schools should include in their behaviour policies. It reminds schools of their legal duties as regards pupils with SEND and lists acceptable forms of sanction. Removal from a classroom is seen as a serious sanction.

Behaviour hubs

In an effort to improve behaviour in school, in 2021 the first cohort of schools joined the DfE's Behaviour Hubs initiative. This is led by Tom Bennett and a team of advisers. A lead school or MAT works with partner schools on diagnosing issues around behaviour in the school and implementing new behaviour approaches. This is a one- or two-year programme of support. There are three streams of support to choose from: Core support, extended support, and MAT support. The programme accepts a new cohort of schools each term. It may be too soon to see how far this approach is improving behaviour in schools, but it could prove useful in helping to reduce low level disruption. This in itself could sort out pupils who are perfectly capable of behaving well but choose not to, from those whose behaviour is a communication of something that needs to be understood and addressed.

North Primary School and Nursery

The first conversation in this chapter is with Alan Garnett, head teacher of North Primary School and Nursery, which is part of a consortium of local primary schools in Colchester. Following the conversation, there is a case study of Alan's school. He mentions being a Rights Respecting School and the effect this has had on the behaviour of the pupils.

Information point: Rights Respecting Schools Award

The Rights Respecting School Award supports schools in embracing the UN Convention on the Rights of the Child (UNCRC). Unicef's award has four standards:

Standard A: Rights-respecting values underpin leadership and management
Standard B: The whole community learns about the Convention
Standard C: The school has a rights-respecting ethos
Standard D: Children are empowered to become active citizens and learners.

Features of a Rights-Respecting classroom include:

- Pupils and staff agree a classroom charter based on rights
- Pupils' views are listened to and are taken into account
- Pupils are able to tell their teachers what they enjoy, what helps them to learn, and to make choices about their learning
- Teachers and teaching assistants (TAs) value and respect each other and other adults
- Teachers avoid the use of "blanket" sanctions when individual pupils have misbehaved
- Staff act as role models by treating each other with respect.

There are three stages: Bronze is the planning stage for moving to the next stage; Silver signifies that UNCRC is becoming embedded in the policy, practice, and culture of the school. Gold is the stage when it is fully embedded in the school's policies, practice, and ethos.

Colchester is one of the towns that became a city in May 2022 as part of the late Queen's Platinum Jubilee celebrations. A diary Alan kept of life as a head teacher during COVID-19 provides a unique account of one head's efforts to cope with a crisis that was unforeseen and outside almost everyone's experience. *A Headteacher's Diary* has been published in the form of a book. The conversation with Alan is followed by a case study of his school.

In conversation with Alan Garnett, head teacher of North Primary School and Nursery, Colchester

Q. Could you tell us something about your school?

A. North School is a primary school in the city centre. Our pupils come from a diverse community, from those who are transient workers or live in social housing, to those who come from places like the Middle East to study for PhDs. Roughly 30% of pupils have English as a second language (EAL) and they speak many different languages. About 25% are entitled to free school meals (FSM) and 20% have SEND.

Q. How do you try to make everyone feel welcome?
        A. We aim to have a culture of inclusion where diversity is seen as an asset. We try to represent different elements of the school community through assemblies and having special events. One of our nursery nurses, for example, is a Muslim and she took an assembly explaining how 20% of her salary goes to help orphan children in Bangladesh. As Easter is celebrated in a unique way in Poland, we had pupils and parents from Poland explaining how it is celebrated. Although I'll always try to recruit the best staff, historically we've managed to have more males teaching in the school, including in infant classes, than is usually the case. We keep in touch with former students who come back to the school to talk to current pupils about the different pathways to adulthood they have taken, including their experiences of university.

Q. How do pupils influence what happens in school?
        A. From Year 2 upwards, each class elects two councillors to represent them on the School Council. Year 5 councillors stay on for two years and are elected as officers: chair, secretary, treasurer, and press officer. The council determines the foci for the year. They have been involved in a sustainable travel project and introduced cycle racks. They were also involved in improving the lunch menus. The local consortium of primary schools has its own Student Council with representatives drawn from all the school councils. This provides an opportunity for members of North's council to take part in discussions and activities with members from the consortium of primary schools across the borough of Colchester to which the school belongs. As well as suggesting improvement to the meals at lunchtimes, the School Council reviews playground rules each year and every pupil is involved in this process and contributes to the quality of the lunchtime play experience. Some Year 5s are playleaders supporting younger children at playtimes. Playleaders are recruited following a formal process which includes writing a letter of application and being interviewed. All those who are appointed receive training for their role. Midday Assistants also help children to find friends when necessary. Some of the older children run clubs at lunchtime and Year 6 pupils have given presentations to prospective parents.

Q. How has being a Rights Respecting School influenced behaviour?
        A. The children know that there are three Rights: The right to feel safe and be safe; the right to respect; and the right to learn. These rights are non-negotiable and are part of our behaviour policy. At the start of every year all classes will have agreed a class charter which will be on display for everyone to see. Teachers talk to new parents and get to know them before any

difficulties arise, which makes it easier if, later on, you have to talk to them about something they don't want to hear. Parents are always kept informed of incidents, as there's nothing worse than not knowing what's going on. The next day, staff will make a beeline for a child who they had helped support after an incident the previous day and show them kindness to let them know they will help to make sure *today will be better*. Little things can be important and make a difference. If pupils are not able to meet our expectations and do not respect others' three rights, we provide guidance and support so that they can independently succeed socially and academically. We try to have a listening culture, which includes teaching children, especially girls, to be assertive and to know when to say "Stop; I don't like it". Pupils should be able to mirror how staff speak to each other, so that everyone is treated with respect.

Q. What rewards do you have?

A. Good Citizens awards are presented in a whole school assembly every Friday. Each teacher nominates children in their own class who have made a positive contribution to the school community. The Midday Assistants nominate one infant and one junior child, too. The ultimate accolades are the Governors Awards. These are presented at the end of each term.

In addition, throughout the year there are tea parties in the Head's office for children who have been nominated by their teachers for an outstanding and sustained commitment to their work. Their parents are invited to celebrate the occasion as well.

Q. How did you manage to write a book during lockdown?

A. If the pandemic had happened early in my headship or if I'd been starting in a new school it would have been ghastly but I have 20 years' experience at North so I had built up a reserve of confidence and trust amongst staff and parents which meant they were generally supportive of my decision-making, even at short notice as we had to react quickly to last minute changes to government guidance. Not having a break for a year and a half – schools remaining open through holidays – meant I was "time rich" to chronicle events!

Q. How did you decide on the book taking the form of a diary?

A. It wasn't my decision to write at all, but I was persuaded to keep a diary by Sir Bob Russell, a former mayor of the town and MP [member of parliament] for Colchester from 1997 to 2015. He and his wife, Lady Russell, have a long association with North School, as their four children attended my school as well as two of their grandchildren. I was already in weekly contact with parents at the school, so every Saturday I put together the information I'd sent them and between us all – parents, staff, pupils and governors – there was always plenty of material. The diary was given a regular column in the *Colchester Daily Gazette*, although my best political jokes were weeded out! I was going to write the diary from March to September 2020, but in the end, I did it for a year.

Q. Did the school close completely at any time?

A. No, we never closed completely. Lockdown 1 was a massive learning curve and staff adapted remarkably quickly to remote teaching and remote pastoral support. [Later on in the pandemic we realised Lockdown 1 was more straightforward to manage because staff did not have to manage teaching and home learning simultaneously – this led to work overload for teachers.] On the first day of lockdown in March 2020, 75 pupils turned up, so I had to make it clear to parents that we were only open for the children of key workers and the numbers went down to around 20. Later, when the definition of "key worker" was extended we had about a quarter of the pupils coming in, which was fine. In fact, we had already invited some children to return where concerns were raised about their emotional health.

Q. What is the school's Free for All charity?

A. This came out of a project with the community to generate income rather than fundraising. Communities working together can make things happen and draw in other organisations to support the school. So far, it has meant that we can provide day trips, swimming and music lessons for every child. We don't want to raise funds for what should be provided, but only to enrich and enhance learning. Classes are involved in business projects too, where they develop their own entrepreneurial skills. Free For All is not about giving the children something for nothing. It's about them learning important life skills: that with teamwork, imagination, creativity, and good old-fashioned hard work, amazing things are possible which will lead to a great sense of fulfilment and achievement, and an education full of rich and diverse experiences that will last in their minds forever.

Case study: North Primary School and Nursery, Colchester

The school was founded in 1894 and caters for 420 pupils. The nursery has places for a further 52 three- and four-year-olds who can attend for either 15 or 30 hours a week. Situated in the centre of Colchester, there is a strong community ethos. Use is made of the links with other educational and sporting facilities to deliver rich and varied learning opportunities.

During its long history, the school has had a series of building projects to enable it to expand and deliver a modern education. As well as four new classrooms, the school has added a music studio, an ICT suite, a community room, a tree room, a gym trail, a vegetable garden, and a woodland play area. As the school has expanded internally and externally, different levels have had to be linked by ramps which meet accessibility requirements. The school's equalities and accessibility plan aims to promote inclusion and community cohesion, so that all aspects of school life can be accessed by pupils, staff, parents, and governors.

The school sees diversity as an asset and a strength which should be both respected and celebrated. Through the work for the Rights Respecting School Award, pupils understand that everyone has a responsibility to be aware of people's rights and to recognise that everyone is of equal value, regardless of their background, culture, or identity. Within the staff team are those who work with EAL pupils, those who support children with speech and language difficulties, or need to use Makaton, as well two staff who are social and emotional health co-ordinators The latter are trained to support children who have been bereaved.

Every child has the opportunity to learn a musical instrument free of charge during the school day. In the infants, children learn rhythm and how to play in a group. In the juniors they have opportunities to learn at least three musical instruments. They put on concerts and the two children in Year 4 who have made the most of these opportunities are awarded music scholarships. These entitle them to free instrument hire and free 1-1 lessons throughout Year 5.

The school has gone out of its way to improve attendance levels, particularly for disadvantaged pupils and those who have SEND. Sunrise and Sunset Clubs provide childcare for pupils before and after school, as well as food and a range of activities. The clubs are run by staff the children know. During lockdown, the school provided 'Grab and Go' lunches for pupils eligible for FSM.

Towards the end of his diary, Alan writes:

> Paradoxically separation has brought us closer together. And that is due to the remarkable people – staff, governors, parents and the children. Let us hope the coming year is just ordinary.
>
> (2021: 162)

It is clear from everything the school does to provide a rich range of learning experiences for the children and the efforts that are made to make everyone feel welcome, that pupils are keen to come to school. This is very much in line with Ken and Kate Robinson's belief that:

> It cannot be overlooked that if children are made to sit for hours on end, day after day, doing work they find uninteresting, for tests they find intimidating, to prepare for some future goal they find uninspiring, that they may fidget and become anxious, stressed or disengaged.
>
> (2022: 58)

Turning next from a school to the kind of support that schools need to be able to draw on, the next section looks at the specialist support services that are needed.

This is especially the case if more pupils are to flourish in mainstream schools rather than needing specialist or alternative provision.

The role of specialist support services

Chapter 2 of this book looked in some detail at the SEND Green Paper. In the third chapter, "Excellent provision from early years to adulthood", there is a section on improving access to specialist support. This begins with the following paragraph:

> Children and young people with SEND frequently require access to additional support from a broad specialist workforce across education, health and care to enable them to effectively access the mainstream curriculum.

(P46: 26)

The next paragraphs go on to list some of the steps the government says it is taking to increase the capacity of the workforce. This includes increasing the number of educational psychologists in training; rolling out the Mental Health Support Teams; and taking action to tackle the waiting times for diagnosis and access to therapies. While it is correct to say these are happening, the scale and pace is another matter.

There is general agreement that more pupils could be supported in mainstream schools if there were sufficient specialist help available that schools could draw on. Despite some LAs managing to retain their specialist support teams, in other areas the help available to schools has dwindled. The next conversation is with Jane Carter, who leads SEND Integrated Services. Before the conversation, there is some information about her work with Di Caesar, retired lead advisory teacher at Gloucestershire County Council. Together, they have raised the profile of professionals working with children and young people who have physical disabilities (PD) through pdnet. They were keen for this to happen, given that there are as many young learners with PD as there are with hearing and visual impairment combined. Yet, as Jane points out, there has not been the same recognition or access to funding. The National Sensory Impairment Partnership (NatSIP) quite rightly has benefited from government funding, as has the Autism Education Trust (AET). However, the last few years has seen the situation for PD improve.

Information point: pdnet

In 2014, the National Network of Advisory Teachers for Physically Impaired Pupils (NNATPIP) changed its name to pdnet, to reflect the changing nature of its membership and to give professionals working in the PD sector a national voice.

Following this change, two one-year DfE contracts enabled pdnet to update its website; develop accredited training courses at levels 1 and 2 for teachers and support staff in early years, schools, and post-16; and to add a growing range of other resources, some of which are free.

These developments have helped the network to grow from 126 members in 2014 to over 7,000 members more recently. This includes LA specialist PD staff, staff in schools and other settings, as well as therapists such as occupational therapists (OTs), physiotherapists, and speech and language therapists. This in itself encourages a multi-professional approach to working with those who have physical difficulties or disabilities.

pdnet operates at both regional and national level. It is a free to join, national network that provides professionals with support in promoting positive outcomes for children and young people with a physical disability and a strong commitment to developing and sharing effective educational practice and pedagogy for learners with PD.

https://pdnet.org.uk

In conversation with Jane Carter, Head of the Integrated Disabilities Service at Warwickshire CC

Q. Could you tell us how you came to be a teacher and what led to your deciding to work in the SEND field?

A. I always wanted to be a teacher and I trained as an English teacher. I became head of the English Department in a secondary school and later a deputy head. My next step was to work for a local authority (LA), where I held a variety of posts before being asked to consider a move into SEN. At that point, I didn't know much about SEN. I was given a copy of the SEN Code of Practice, and thrown in at the deep end. Luckily, I had a great mentor who went on to lead the SEN service in another LA. With her support and the trust of the CEO, I learnt the hard way. It taught me that if you know how to lead and manage, knowledge and understanding can follow.

Q. Could you explain how your current role with the Integrated Disability Service fits in to the LA's overall structure?

A. In 2019–20, the LA went through a transformation of its education services, dividing them into those who commission and those who deliver. Within the delivery arm is the Educational Psychology Service and the SEND and Inclusion Services. The later includes: the Specialist Teaching Service (STS); the Ethnic Minority Achievement Service (EMAS); the Flexible Learning Team (FLT) which supports those missing school due to ill health; and the Integrated Disability Service (IDS). This brings together professionals from education working in partnership with other professionals to provide a range of services to support children in their early years, and children and young people with low incidence needs at home, early years settings, and schools. One contact opens the door to a range of different teams.

Q. What do you provide for pre-school children and their families and is your work linked with Family Hubs?

A. Within this structure, the 0–5 years Team includes staff trained to deliver Portage, the home-visiting educational service for pre-school children with SEND and their families. Historically the 0–5 Team has delivered parent training but we are in the process of working with staff from the Family Hubs to capacity build, so some of the more specialist training can be delivered from there alongside their universal parent training.

Our Area SENCOs working in the early years have post-graduate qualifications in autism, speech & language, and educational audiology. The team also includes those who have the mandatory training for teachers of the deaf and for the visually impaired, as well as manual handling trainers, Makaton Regional trainers, and NAS EarlyBird trainers.

Q. What range of specialisms does your team cover and how do schools draw on your services? Do MATs have their own arrangements?

A. Whereas the 0–5 team covers all areas of SEND, the School Age Team currently concentrates on PD, hearing impairment (HI), multi-sensory impairment (MSI) and complex needs. Visual impairment (VI) is also covered but this is commissioned from a special school. Schools don't have to pay for specialist teacher input for low incidence SEND.

In the case of the Specialist Teaching Service (STS), schools who subscribe and buy a day a week or fortnight will have a designated specialist teacher who will provide most of that school's specialist advice, such as: a strategic audit, a review of training for staff, assessments and observations of individual learners, access arrangements, and strategic SENCO support. Several STS teachers have the SENCO qualification, so a school faced with a maternity leave or an unplanned absence can buy a SENCO service.

The PD/Complex Need Team supports learners in mainstream schools with a range of conditions. In addition to the higher incidence conditions, such as Down syndrome, cerebral palsy, and foetal alcohol spectrum disorder, the team is supporting children with a number of rare syndromes and those whose difficulties stem from extreme prematurity (ie being born at 23 weeks).

As far as MATs are concerned, some do make their own arrangements and some schools buy services from independent companies, including sole traders. The difficulty for these schools is that their professionals aren't linked in to the LA's policies and processes.

Q. To what extent does your team work with professionals from across education, health, and social care?

A. Frontline staff have excellent working relationships on the ground. In one area we are co-located with OTs, physios and the Pre-school Autism Service. I work almost daily with our Designated Clinical Officer (DCO), who by profession is a consultant nurse. He will give advice on diabetes management, epilepsy, and medication issues in schools and other settings, such as whether an intervention requires a health member of staff or whether a TA can be trained to carry it out. Issues arise when something is too complex for the Universal School Nursing Service, but the child isn't known to the local Children's Community Nursing Team. It may be that the child has a specialist nurse at a regional hospital, but the school needs to know where to go for advice.

I've seen a significant improvement in the last two years around social care and SEND. When my staff have concerns and ask me to escalate, my equivalent in social care is extremely responsive and acknowledges the expertise and judgement of my staff.

Being able to communicate remotely, through Microsoft Teams and other platforms, has improved inter-agency working considerably and attendance at meetings has improved. We have recently introduced Early Help surgery drop-ins, so that staff in FLT and STS can get advice from Early Help professionals if they need to.

Q. From a pdnet perspective, is there anything else you would have liked to have seen in the SEND Green Paper?

A. Although the Green Paper accepts that the level of confidence amongst teachers in supporting children with SEND is low and appropriate training around SEND has significantly decreased, there is no reference as to how the DfE proposes to address this in relation to low incidence SEND. Page 46 of the Green Paper does say that steps are being taken to increase the capacity of the specialist workforce, but this is extremely limited in scope. How will this be addressed in relation to HI, VI, MSI, and PD in the context of an ageing and reducing workforce with no central funding for specialist qualifications? pdnet has previously provided evidence to the DfE on the erosion of specialist LA Physical Disability Support Teams. Even those areas still with PD specialist teachers are not being replaced as they retire. The hierarchy created by the historic mandatory qualifications for HI, VI, and MSI results in children and young people with PD or autism not having access to specialist advice, yet their needs are equally complex and frequently misunderstood.

There needs to be greater clarity as to leadership expectations and accountabilities at every level, with levers in the system for ensuring each fulfils their role as regards to children and young people with SEND. All too often, too much is expected of a SENCO, whose status may be insufficient to influence the quality of teaching, hence the current issues with poor outcomes and inconsistency of provision at SEN support. Raising the status of the SENCO and having clear expectations about protected non-contact time for them would help with recruitment and retention. In Warwickshire half of the secondary SENCOs have changed in the last twelve months. The proposed national standards, therefore, need to consider mandating the SENCO's position on the leadership team. National standards must also be drawn up with the relevant sector specialists, such as NatSIP, BATOD, pdnet, AET. How will adherence to national standards be monitored and quality assured? Will this be through Ofsted inspections or broader accountability via LAs and regional directors? Should a setting, for example, be prevented from getting anything higher than 'requires improvement' if they are unable to evidence adherence to the standards?

Q. Your LA was involved in piloting the new Area SEND Framework. How did it go?

A. I was impressed by the thoroughness of the Senior HMI and her willingness to listen to suggestions. It was interesting to see how there is a shift from the previous framework to paying more attention to the views of young people and their parents. They are on the receiving end of services and know what is working well and what needs to improve. The same is true of frontline staff who are in a position to tell it as it is.

In one of her final comments, Jane referred to three organisations: AET is the Autism Education Trust; BATOD is the British Association of Teachers of the Deaf; and NatSIP is the National Association for Sensory Impairment.

Exclusions

The final of the three themes in this chapter is about school exclusions. There used to be fixed term and permanent exclusion. More recently, this has been changed to suspension and exclusion. Following the joint consultation mentioned at the start of this chapter, the latest guidance was issued in September 2022. In the opening paragraph, the DfE states that:

> Good behaviour in schools is essential to ensure that all pupils benefit from the opportunities provided by education. Therefore, the government recognises that school exclusions, managed moves and off-site direction are essential behaviour management tools for headteachers and can be used to establish high standards of behaviour in schools and maintain the safety of school communities.
>
> (2022d: 3)

The guidance clarifies the role of head teachers, governing boards, and LAs. Part 10 covers the roles of all those involved when there has to be an Independent Review Panel (IRP). The next conversation is with Diana Robinson who is an SEN Expert. This role originates from *The School Discipline (Pupil Exclusions and Reviews) (England) Regulations 2012* and is also explained in the DfE's Exclusions Guidance 2017 and 2022.

Information point: Independent Review Panels and the SEN Expert

Governors Disciplinary Panel (GDP) Following a head teacher's decision to exclude, a panel of governors meets to decide whether to decline to reinstate the pupil, or to direct reinstatement of the pupil immediately or on a particular date.

Independent Review Panel (IRP) If they decline to reinstate the pupil, the parents have the right to request a review of the governing board's decision and an IRP is set up. This is made up of governors who were not on the GDP.

Parents The parents have the right to request the involvement of an SEN Expert who is appointed by the LA. As it is important that parents have confidence in the person's ability to be both capable and impartial, the SEN Expert must be a professional with first-hand experience of pupils with SEN, such as an educational psychologist, a SENCO, or a specialist teacher, including those who have recently retired from these positions.

The SEN Expert The SEN expert, along with the governors on the IRP, has copies of all the paperwork leading up to the head teacher's decision to exclude, as well as the minutes and any other evidence of how the governors who made up the GDP came to the decision to decline to reinstate the excluded pupil.

The IRP's decision The IRP can uphold the decision to exclude; recommend that the GDP reconsiders its decision not to reinstate the pupil; or quash their decision and direct that the governing board reconsiders reinstatement. They can also order a financial adjustment of £4000 to be paid to the LA if they receive a "quash and reconsider" judgement and fail to reinstate the pupil.

The SEN Expert's role is not to examine the original decision to exclude, but to see if the governors, in coming to their decision, had given due consideration to their legal duties under the Equality Act 2010 and the 2014 Children and Families Act. In addition, the SEN expert can advise on whether or not sufficient consideration had been given to the pupil's recognised SEN, or to the possibility that they had unidentified needs which, in either case, could have had a bearing on the exclusion.

In conversation with Diana Robinson, SEN Expert

Q. Could you explain your background and what led up to your becoming an SEN Expert?

A. I began my career in education as an art teacher in a secondary school. I also did some supply work in primary schools and decided I preferred it, because you're teaching a class of pupils rather than teaching a subject. I worked my way up to being a senior teacher and then the head of a small primary school followed by being head of a larger one. After completing an MA (SEN) at Canterbury Christ Church University, I joined the Advisory Service in Kent where I worked for almost 20 years, providing advisory support for special schools and mainstream schools with specialist resource provisions. During this time, I completed Ofsted training (although I haven't kept it up), and the School Improvement Partner (SIP) accreditation training. Although you can have direct influence as a head, the advisory work meant making slightly more strategic decisions that might improve the system as a whole. For many years, I've also been a member of Prospect, the union for UK professionals in the public and private sectors, where I enjoy being part of their Education and Children's Services Group Executive Council.

Q. Tell us about your role as an SEN Expert and what is involved?

A. I've been an SEN Expert since the role was introduced as part of the changes to exclusions regulations in 2012. On average, I do about 10 to 15 cases a year so I've done quite a number since I started. The purpose of the SEN Expert is to have an impartial person, who hasn't been involved in the case, looking at the correctness of the governors' decision-making. To do this, we consider three aspects: illegality, irrationality, and impropriety. It's a paper-based exercise. I don't meet the child or do any assessments, but I receive the full bundle of papers the governors have received including the minutes of the GDP meeting. This means that, as SEN Experts, we can see if both the Children and Families Act and the Equality Act 2010 have been applied. The guidance on exclusions is quite clear that governors must apply both Acts. Without knowing their duties under these Acts, governors can make the wrong decisions. It is not our role to pass judgement on the original decision made by the head teacher, but only to examine the governors' decision-making process. It's important that the parents of the child feel confident that governors weren't prejudiced in any way.

Q. Do you think governors understand their responsibilities sufficiently?

A. Governors who make up a GDP and a different set of governors who form the IRP, need to understand how a child's underlying needs can affect the way they behave. I have concerns that not all governors will be aware of how a pupil's condition can affect their behaviour, including the fact that they may not knowingly be breaking any rules, but lack the understanding or the control to observe them. If it's deliberate, that's one thing, but that's not always the case. There are far too many cases of children being excluded because of breaking school rules which seem rather petty such as being too strict about the school's dress code.

It's been noticeable that of the many cases I've dealt with where the decision has been to quash the decision of the GDP, almost all have involved pupils in mainstream schools. This may not be surprising given that governors of these schools will not necessarily have had much involvement with SEND pupils.

Q. Could you give us some examples of why appeals are quashed?

A. Mostly they are quashed because the governors involved have inadequate knowledge of the Equality Act and the Children and Families Act. The first of these Acts introduced the term "reasonable adjustments", which refers to adjustments that should be made for pupils with SEND, while the Equality Act sets out that disabled pupils or others who have protected characteristics should not be discriminated against.

Sometimes, governors haven't asked any questions about SEN or disability, particularly where the school states that the pupil does not have SEN. In these cases they can be criticised if they don't invite their SENCO to attend the hearing to explain how they know there is no SEN when, for instance, there has been a history of persistent disruptive behaviour which could indicate an unmet need. It's important that governors satisfy themselves that the correct provision has been made and don't just accept the head's word for it.

Another example is where the facts of the incident show that a serious assault occurred with a pupil known to have special needs, but who hadn't received any interventions or strategies. This indicated that neither the school's SEN policy or the 2015 SEND Code of Practice was being complied with. As every school must use their "best endeavours" to make sure that a child with SEN gets the support they need, then the GDP may decide the school has not used their best endeavours. In this case, they should reinstate the pupil because the school may have contributed to the incident by not making the right provision.

One rather unusual case occurred when I was sent the usual bundle of papers, but one of the reports only had every other page printed, as, whoever had been doing the photocopying, had failed to realise the original report had been written on both sides of the page! I realise the cases I get to see are the ones where governors have not done the right thing – not the ones where they do.

Q. Have there been many changes to the latest exclusions guidance?

A. No, the latest guidance, which came into force in September 2022, is much the same as the 2017 version. There is more about "managed moves" being agreed between schools so that a pupil can make a fresh start at another school rather than being excluded. Also, there is more about the use of "off-site direction" which often means some form of alternative provision. It worries me that the latter can be arranged without the parents having any say about it. I don't think there's enough support or involvement for parents. Going to the SEN Tribunal is another example. It's all left to the parents to know how to go about it.

Q. What do you think needs to change in education?

A. For a start, there is far too much testing and I don't think it's good for the pupils. It may be considered to be part of accountability, but the wrong people get hurt by it. My greatest concern, however, is that governance isn't given enough importance. Being a head teacher is a powerful position, but heads need a strong governing board to support them. I've seen so many occasions when governors don't challenge the head teacher, but rubber stamp what they say without question. Governors need a better understanding of their role and its significance. In relation to my role as an SEN Expert, I think it's a real oversight that nothing is published about the decisions IRPs come to, so nothing is shared and lessons aren't learned. In all the roles I've had, even with being an SEN Expert where you may never meet the pupil, it's the same: you need not only to like children, you need to like *these* children.

In her final answer, along with saying that governors need more training to understand their role in exclusions and to be able to question the information they receive from the head, Diana refers to her concern that there is too much testing of pupils and this is taken up as one of the themes in the next chapter.

Alternative Provision

It was quite a surprise to many when the SEND Green Paper was predicated upon there being a single SEND and AP system. Although the majority of APs work with pupils who are excluded, it was explained earlier in this book that AP also educates pupils who are out of school for other reasons. The next conversation is with Timothy Ellis, who leads the work of Leamington LAMP. This is a provision for older students who have not been excluded, but who, due to extreme anxieties, have been out of education, sometimes for years, and who respond to a calmer, more creative approach to the curriculum. During the conversation, Timothy mentions Biodata sonification.

Information point: Biodata sonification

Biodata sonification is the process of extracting real time biological information from living plants. Biodata sonification devices are able to convert minute electrical signals in humans – and plants – and convert them into useful musical control voltage.

Plants can play synthesisers by sending tiny electronic pulses to a module that converts them. The sounds themselves are programmed by a human, but the system will be silent until it is connected to a plant using sticky electrode pads.

As well as translating micro currents from plants into sensory music, this can be taken a stage further by plugging humans in to the system to form a duo or trio with a plant.

In this way, plant music is a creative collaboration between humans and plants.

People who say they do not like synthesisers usually change their mind when seeing them used in this way.

In conversation with Timothy Ellis, Strategic Lead at Leamington LAMP

Q. When was LAMP established; how many students can you cater for; and what is the age range?

A. I set up one of the first AP centres in Northamptonshire in 1999 and Leamington LAMP was established in 2013. We currently have 50 part time students (5% increase each year). The age range is 14–19.

Q. How many of your students have EHC plans, a diagnosis of autism, or have been excluded?

A. All the students have EHC plans and they would be classed as neurodiverse – 95% have autism diagnosis. None had been excluded, but they dropped out of mainstream due to trauma/extreme anxiety.

Q. Are you able to select which students come to LAMP?

A. We can't select students directly but we work closely with the LA and families to determine if they are the right fit for LAMP.

Q. How do you make the environment more appropriate for those with high levels of anxiety?

A. The place doesn't look like a school or college, as you enter it's more like an art centre. Staff and students dress to be comfortable (no suits or ties). Staff and students use first names and we don't have a staff room – we all share the lounge area.

Q. Could you explain why creativity is at the heart of your curriculum and how you deliver it in practice?

A. We believe that promoting creative output is critical for maintaining wellbeing. Creative activities are an opportunity to express ideas. Expressing ideas and seeing them develop gives young people a sense of achievement, a feeling that they are being taken seriously and their ideas are important. Access to high quality creative activity can make the difference between a happy child and an unhappy one. Being happy will help someone engage with a full curriculum.

Q. Where did you come across biodata sonification and how have you developed it with your students?

A. I developed an interest in modular synthesisers following trials during music enrichment work with young autistic students. It became clear that some young people responded very positively to being given full control over sound design decisions in a physical way (rather than using a mouse in a computer system). The modular system has its patch connection points accessible on the front panel rather than hidden away inside. We approach sound design through the idea of sounds as moods – this approach led us to develop ideas around self-generated sensory music.

When researching new ways to interact with the modular system, we heard about using sensors to pick up the microscopic electrical pulses in living things, for instance plants. Some students will "plug themselves in" using clips on the ear lobes or fingers, so that their own biodata will trigger the system – like a human sequencer. I'm not aware of any other schools/agencies doing this work with young people. But we'd welcome the opportunity to take the ideas out and about to other settings.

Q. The SEND Green Paper says it is about creating a single SEND and AP system. Do you agree with this approach?

A. The risk with a single SEND and AP system is that it has the potential to be inflexible, which defeats the unique selling point (USP) of AP for learners who require a differentiated approach. That said, the lack of a joined up system (particularly around reporting) has had huge detriment in terms of what we know about the impact of AP. The DfE doesn't even have an accurate record of the number of young people who access AP.

Q. The Green Paper sets out five outcomes for AP schools. Could you say how far you think each one these would be a useful measure in general, or for your school: effective outreach support; improved attendance; reintegration; academic attainment with a focus on English and maths; successful post-16 transitions?

A. As with all measures, outreach really depends on how it works in practice. Inadequate outreach is one of the main reasons placements fail, but the risk with this measure is ensuring loopholes aren't created that can allow for gaming the system. Our outreach work is targeted at students whose attendance dramatically dips and this is where outreach work is effective in leading to increased attendance.

Overall attendance is a useful measure for how successful a placement is. The risk here is that it could lead to settings being unwilling to start working with a young person who they see as a potential low attender, especially when this is due to reasons outside the influence of the setting, such as ongoing health conditions.

As regards attainment, the secondary education reforms in the mid-2010s as regards attainment (Progress 8/Attainment 8) focused primarily on the progress children and young people made, with attainment being a secondary measure. It's disappointing that nearly ten years later, attainment is being suggested as a primary focus, without reference to progression, especially with SEND learners, many of whom will have lower attainment than their peers regardless of their provision.

Successful transitions are obviously an important part of a young person's journey through education, but this measure risks being short-term data that doesn't tell the whole story. A more effective measure would be the destination of a young person two, three, and four years after they have transitioned from the setting, to measure the long-term effectiveness of preparations for adulthood and resilience.

Q. What links do you have with health and with social care? How many of your students need support from these services as well as from education?

A. Our links are via regional and local frameworks and referral processes. We take part in inter-agency working as required to meet the students' needs. All our students require support from one or both of these services.

Q. What relationships or partnerships do you have with: other APs, local secondary schools, and the local community?

A. Most of our referrals are through the LA SEN teams and from time to time other APs will refer a young person to us, who wants to engage in a particular subject that we offer. Some regional secondary schools also refer to us independently from the LA. Students will remain on the roll at the mainstream school and attend LAMP part time. We operate additional funded projects, such as concerts and arts festivals, that give our students the opportunity to gain work experience and also for the local community to see what we're doing, how our students are achieving, and also to take part in some exciting, original art activities.

Conclusions

This chapter has explored the links between attendance, behaviour, and exclusion and how all three themes rely on close working with families as well as interagency working. This way of working is also vital for pupils who are in AP, whether or not they have been excluded. The next chapter is similar in being based round four case studies and conversations which focus more on special school provision and encompass the themes of testing and assessment, from the early years to post-16, as part of the government's drive to wipe out illiteracy and innumeracy.

References

DfE (2022) *Sustainability in High Needs Systems: Guidance for Local Authorities*. Available from Local authority guidance on high needs sustainability (publishing.service.gov.uk)

Garnett, A. (2021) *A Headteacher's Diary*. Colchester: Red Lion Books.

Gov.Uk (2012) *The School Discipline (Pupil Exclusions and Reviews) (England) Regulations (2012)*. Available from https://www.legislation.gov.uk/uksi/2012/1033/made

Gov.Uk (2017) *Exclusion from Maintained Schools, Academies and Pupil Referral Units in England*. Available from https://consult.education.gov.uk/school-absence-and-exclusions-team/statutory-exclusion-guidance/supporting_documents/Draft%20statutory%20guidance%202017.pdf

Gov.Uk (2019) *Timpson Review of School Exclusion*. Available from https://assets.publishing.service.gov.uk/government/uploads/system/uploads/attachment_data/file/807862/Timpson_review.pdf

Gov.UK (2022a) *Behaviour in Schools Advice for Headteachers and School Staff*. Available from https://consult.education.gov.uk/school-absence-and-exclusions-team/revised-school-behaviour-and-exclusion-guidance/supporting_documents/Behaviour%20in%20schools%20%20advice%20for%20headteachers%20and%20school%20staff.pdf

Gov.UK (2022b) *Opportunity for All: Strong Schools with Great Teachers for Your Child*. Available from https://www.gov.uk/government/publications/opportunity-for-all-strong-schools-with-great-teachers-for-your-child

Gov.UK (2022c) SEND Review: Right Support, Right Place, Right Time. Available from https://assets.publishing.service.gov.uk/government/uploads/system/uploads/attachment_data/file/1063620/SEND_review_right_support_right_place_right_time_accessible.pdf

Gov.UK (2022d) *Suspension and Permanent Exclusion from maintained schools, academies and pupil referral units in England, including pupil movement* from https://assets.publishing.service.gov.uk/government/uploads/system/uploads/attachment_data/file/1101498/Suspension_and_Permanent_Exclusion_from_maintained_schools__academies_and_pupil_referral_units_in_England__including_pupil_movement.pdf

Gov.UK (2022e) *Working Together to Improve School Attendance.* Available from https://www.gov.uk/government/publications/working-together-to-improve-school-attendance

https://www.childrenscommissioner.gov.uk/help-at-hand/

pdnet https://pdnet.org.uk

Robinson Sir K., and K. Robinson (2022) *Imagine If…: Creating a Future for Us All.* London: Penguin Books.

Unicef https://www.unicef.org.uk/rights-respecting-schools/

6   Meeting the needs of a minority

> What is beyond doubt is that there is a growing continuum of provision, that special schools after years of isolation are thoroughly embedded in the school system and that the more people find ways of working together across schools, across services and with parents and families, the more likely it is that answers will be found as to how to reach and teach every child and young person, no matter how complex their needs.
>
> (Tutt 2016: 117)

The previous chapter looked at the provision for children in mainstream schools and the support they need to be able draw on from across the services. This chapter has examples of four specialist settings. The first is a secondary school for pupils with a variety of learning needs and the second is an all-age day and residential school for deaf chldren. The final two settings are both specialist multi-academy trusts (MATs). One is maintained by the state and the other is a charitable trust. Following the linked themes in the last chapter of attendance, behaviour, and exclusion, this chapter considers the government's emphasis on pupils reaching age-related expectations and what it means in the context of children and young people who experience a range of barriers to learning, some of which are surmountable and some of which will always be present.

Expected standards

As mentioned in Chapter 1 of this book, one of the missions in the Levelling Up White Paper said that, *"By 2030, 90% of primary children will achieve the expected standard in reading, writing and maths"*. This was repeated in the Schools White Paper, but with the addition of increasing the average GCSE grade in English language and maths, from 4.5 to 5. It was pointed out then, and is reiterated here, that talking about expectations of reaching certain standards at set ages is not inducive to helping all children to feel, and to be, included. In Chapter 4 of this book, there were examples of pupils who were cognitively very able, but whose outlook was bleak until they were able to flourish in a setting where their significant needs were understood and met. Significantly, this was through the involvement of health and social care as well as education. In this chapter, there are individual case

DOI: 10.4324/9781003333203-9

studies of children whose low cognitive ability is combined with other factors and where the real progress they made had no relevance in terms of trying to get them to an "expected standard". This inflexible approach leads to trying to fit pupils into a system of schooling that exists, rather than making sure the system will fit every young learner.

Meeting different needs

There is no doubt that, over time, the pupil population has become more complex. There are many reasons for this. Societal changes have led to more young people having less stable backgrounds. Social media has changed the nature of childhood and not always for the better.

The impact of these and many other rapid changes nationally and internationally have resulted in an increasing number of children and young people experiencing mental health issues. This upward trend was noted even before the pandemic. In 2017, the DoH and the DfE published *Transforming Children and Young People's Mental Health Provision: A Green Paper*. Although, as yet, this has not led to a Bill, the main concepts in it are being rolled out, albeit very slowly, as described elsewhere in this book. While concerns about young people's mental health and wellbeing have been widely recognised (ie Tutt and Williams 2021), there has been an increase in the complexity of the pupils now in school for other reasons as well, including premature babies surviving at an even earlier stage of their development; also, the number of rare syndromes is growing, as is the number of children being diagnosed with co-existing conditions.

The Valley School, Stevenage

The first case study begins with a conversation with David Pearce, head teacher at The Valley School. In the conversation, David mentions Enemy of Boredom, a locally available alternative provision (AP).

Information point: EOB Academy

The Enemy of Boredom (EOB) Academy was created by Steve Godwin as a place where young people can learn together and learn from each other, through the medium of video gaming and esports. Based in Bracknell, it has centres in Letchworth and Baldock, as well as being accessible online.

The academy runs courses specifically for young people with an EHC plan. Not only does it engage them in learning in a way that appeals to them, but it can lead to qualifications and access to a variety of jobs in the industry, such as working alongside game designers, computer programmers, animators, software developers, and audio engineers.

EOB Academy's partnership with the Prince's Trust has been in action since 2017.

In conversation with David Pearce, Head of The Valley School

Q. What made you decide that teaching was what you wanted to do?

A. When I was a pupil my favourite lesson was PE (physical education). I was good at sport and the PE teacher made the lessons so enjoyable, they didn't feel like lessons. I went on to do a sports degree because I enjoyed the subject, but with no clear idea of what I wanted to do next. I needed to get a job as the money had run out, so I joined the police force, even though I still wasn't sure what career I wanted to follow. It was while I was working as a police officer, that I realised the need to intervene and to make a difference in young people's lives before it's too late. So I took a Postgraduate Certificate in Education (PGCE) course and went into teaching. Although teaching can be tough, I've never felt it was work but rather a labour of love and I was blessed to be able to do it.

Q. What made you switch to special education after teaching in mainstream secondary schools?

A. It was after meeting up with a professional footballer from a difficult background who, growing up, thought he'd never be able to become a professional, until he was told by one of his teachers, *"It's not where you come from, but where you're going to and that's up to you"*. Pupils in special schools have many difficulties to overcome, so that's where you can make the most difference. I'm amazed by some students' joy and happiness, even after experiencing so much adversity. At The Valley School, we try to promote positivity, achievement, and success.

Q. Since becoming a head, what would you say is your leadership style, or has it changed depending on the type of school you're running?

A. Having one style of leadership would be boring. I think of it like having a set of golf clubs and being able to pull out the right one for the situation. Sometimes you have to be directional and more autocratic, for instance where safeguarding is concerned. At other times, you can stand back and be like a shepherd pointing the sheep in the right direction. If leading a school out of an Ofsted category, you may need to be more autocratic; in other schools, you can be more democratic. I don't think leadership is about knowing more than everyone else, it is about finding the right answer from the room, utilizing the skills and talents of those around you.

Q. As someone who's had experience of joining a MAT, why did your previous school make that choice?

A. There were two reasons. Firstly, I took over a school that hadn't received a good Ofsted judgement. So it was a question of becoming an academy and joining a MAT before the choice was made for us and we were pushed. Secondly, we already had links with our feeder school, which was a primary school for for pupils with social, emotional, and mental health difficulties (SEMH). As we were the secondary equivalent, it was more like becoming an all-age school. Our chair of governors described it as being like a marriage of love and not a forced marriage!

Q. The Schools Bill currently going through parliament is keen on academisation. Do you think being part of a MAT is the right way forward for every school?

A. This should be a localised decision made with the governors, the Senior Leadership Team (SLT), staff, and parents. It must show how joining a MAT would add value. Simply adding another layer of bureaucracy is not necessarily helpful and takes money away from pupils in order to pay for the CEO's salary, office space, PA (personal assistant), etc. In my experience, this can take over £100k per annum out of the classroom.

Q. The SEND Green Paper talks of a SEND and alternative provision system. How do you see this working?

A. A formalised approach is good, as long as enough time is given to implement it properly; that it isn't done on the cheap; and everyone knows what the outcomes should be. It is important to start with the outcome, what we want to achieve for the child first, and then decide on the system for getting there. It also needs continuity from start to finish of a new system being put in place, without a change of leadership in the middle which causes problems.

Q. What has been your experience of the obstacles in working with health and with social care to meet the needs of young learners and how have you overcome these?

A. The main obstacles are the same for both: their heavy workload, the size of their caseload, and the time at their disposal. The really frustrating thing is that, in an hour's session, they may spend 20 minutes with the child and 40 minutes writing their report. I haven't found the answer, but I do know that it is a waste of their time to have to write up reports, which is something admin could do. If they had help with this, they could spend more time with each pupil leading to better outcomes for pupils and a better use of their time.

Q. As special schools often have a wider catchment area than local schools, how have you encouraged parents to feel part of the school community?

A. Firstly, because I'm dealing with fewer families than would be the case in most mainstream schools, I can be more accessible and I encourage my SLT to be the same. If they want a visit, whether as a prospective parent or a current one, I try to make sure it's arranged within seven days. It's amazing how some of these visits change parents' perceptions of what goes on in a special school. Many tell me they are surprised by finding there is a calm atmosphere when they were expecting it to be chaotic!

Every week, I produce an illustrated newsletter, so that parents know what is going on and we try to keep our website up to date and encourage them to use it. As well as a number of events every term, we invite all the parents of pupils who have just joined us from their primary schools to come in at lunchtime and sit with their children and the staff who teach them, so that they can talk about how they're settling in to Year 7.

Q. You've made quite a few changes to the curriculum recently. What do you hope it will achieve?

A. The curriculum is student-led, meaning that it changes with the needs of the pupils, so there is stretch and challenge for everyone whatever level they are working at. We see it as greenhousing rather than warehousing, so that staff will be enthusiastic about what they're teaching. This engages the students and both are empowered. They won't be bored but achieving. These adapted approaches to learning at all levels means no one feels they are bottom of the class because they will be working with pupils who are at a similar level. This leads to improved behaviour and means they make progress. We all want students to know more and be able to do more when they leave us. This helps prepare them to be successful in the next chapter in their learning journey.

Q. You've worked with many pupils who may have been poor attenders, or whose behaviour meant they were excluded. How have you improved attendance and reduced exclusions?

A. Start from where the child is and build relationships with the child and the family. I want to run an outward-looking school. We have a family engagement worker, who, depending on what diet a child needs to help them to engage in education, will start by teaching in the child's home or on neutral ground away from the school, via the internet, or using locally available AP. This includes Enemy of Boredom, which gives young people access to learn about video game creation and esports, or gain a BTEC (Business and Technology Education Council) in computing. We also use animal therapy in the form of equine therapy. A third AP provider offers the opportunity to gain experience in boat building and carpentry. Sometimes pupils are on our roll, but have been out of school for as long as two years, so something different must be offered, because we can't expect them to rock up to school as normal in September or whenever they're due to start. It is important that staff feel they have the freedom to adopt novel approaches to teaching and learning, and that the small, incremental successes can be celebrated.

Q. Is there anything you would like to add?

A. Staff who want to work in special schools must understand the challenges. At present, trainee teachers aren't taught much about SEND or have opportunities to see what special schools offer. We're the poor relations in terms of training. This means we get applications from teachers who want to care for pupils who have special needs, rather than focus on how to support their learning and development. This won't change until the content of their training prepares them to work with pupils who have varying types of need, together with ensuring that time spent in special schools are part of their training.

Following the conversation with David Pearce, the case study focuses on how the school has moved from seeing interventions as being delivered mainly on an individual basis to taking a whole school approach. The SENCO, Elaine McWilliams, takes the information in pupils' EHC plans to look at the approaches all pupils need and the pupils who require individual interventions as well. Some of the more recent approaches she mentions are described in the following Information point.

Information point: Interventions at The Valley School

Colourful Semantics This approach was developed by Alison Bryan, a speech and language therapist (SaLT) specialising in language disorders. She has devised a way of helping children to understand grammar by breaking down sentences into their component parts before putting them together again. It starts with four key colours: WHO – orange; WHAT DOING – yellow; WHAT – Green; WHERE – BLUE. There are further stages for adverbs, adjectives, conjunctions, and negatives.

https://www.integratedtreatmentservices.co.uk/our-approaches/speech-therapy-approaches/colourful-semantics-2/

The SHAPE CODING system was designed by SaLT Dr Susan Ebbels at Moor House School & College, to teach spoken and written grammar to school-aged children with Developmental Language Disorder (DLD).

https://shapecoding.com

Visual Coding is a hybrid of **Colourful Semantics** and the **Shape Coding**™ **System** and is used by SaLT teams to enable students to recognise the word classes by shape and colour. This has been adopted as a whole school intervention/approach at The Valley School.

Talk for Writing This has been developed by Pie Corbett, a prolific writer who has inspired many teachers. The approach encourages pupils to think about the language they need to use before starting to write. To move from dependence to a greater degree of independence, schools need to make sure pupils have experienced a wide range of fiction, non-fiction, and poetry. This approach enables children to imitate orally the language they need for a particular topic, before reading and analysing it, and then writing their own version.

https://www.talk4writing.com/https://www.talk4writing.com/about/

The Valley School, along with many other similar schools nationally, is no longer described as a school for pupils who have moderate learning difficulties (MLD). At one stage, MLD schools were redesignated by the LA as being for pupils with learning difficulties; autism; and speech, language, and communication needs (SLCN). These schools are now described in the LA's local offer as being for pupils who have learning disabilities (LD). The LA has kept separate schools for severe learning difficulties and profound & multiple learning difficulties (SLD & PMLD); social, emotional, and mental health difficulties (SEMH); physical and neurological impairment (PNI); and hearing impairment (HI). The LA is also adding to its list of specialist resource provisions attached to mainstream schools.

Case study: The Valley School, Stevenage

The Valley School is a secondary school for pupils who have a range of learning needs. Currently in a building that is no longer fit for purpose, during 2023 the school will move into a new building on the same site when it will be able to accommodate 175 students.

There are three classes in each year group. Elaine has adapted the use of a hub and spoke model to create a central Interventions Hub with a Hublet for each year group. These are calm, breakout spaces for interventions and for progressing EHCP targets.

The whole school has adopted the Zones of Regulation intervention, so that students can recognise and name their emotions and describe how they are feeling. To remind students to use this approach, staff wear lanyards with the zones on them and classrooms have zones check-in stations. Other whole school interventions centre round friendship and social skills; protective behaviours; consent; and sensory needs, which are delivered through the Interventions Team by covering a Personal, social, health and economic education (PSHE) teaching session.

In each of the Year Group Hublets, the following are delivered:

- Colourful Semantics
- LEGO therapy
- Speech and language therapy (SaLT)
- Support for gross and fine motor skill activities
- Talk for Writing
- Zones of Regulation

A further hublet is the Outreach Support Hublet, which delivers: in-home tutoring; online learning; family visits; family support; parent workshops; SEND lending library; and referrals to outside agencies.

Elaine has worked closely with the head of English and with the school's speech and language therapist in developing the overall approach.

As the LA was one of the early trailblazers for mental health support teams (MHSTs) arising from the Mental Health Green Paper, the school benefits from having an education mental health practitioner (EMHP). She visits the school regularly, working closely with Elaine who is training to become the school's Senior Mental Health Lead (SMHL) as well as SENCO. As the teaching team are released from a PSHE session that the Interventions Team lead on, the intention is for that time to be used to develop awareness and proficiency in a range of interventions and strategies to promote good mental health and wellbeing.

As an update to the Mental Health Green Paper, the DfE published **Transforming Children and Young People's Mental Health Implementation Programme**. This showed that 98% of SMHLs were combining it with other significant roles. Of those who had applied for a grant to cover the training, 30% were the safeguarding lead; 22% were SENCOs; and 19% were the pastoral lead. In addition, the role was carried out by head teachers, deputies, and assistant heads. While it may make sense for SMHLs to be senior figures in the school, it adds considerably to their workload.

Deaf Education

Before the next case study about provision for deaf children, there is some general information about the controversies that have surrounded the education of these pupils.

It has been mentioned previously in this book, that one of the defining characteristics of children and young people who have SEND, is that many need support from health and social care as well as from education. This is certainly true of those who come under the broad category of having sensory and/or physical needs. This includes those who are described in the SEND Code of Practice 2015 as having vision impairment, hearing impairment, or multi-sensory impairment. Along with those who have a physical disability, they are likely to need significant input from the health service and often from social services as well. This is another example of how important it is to work across professional boundaries in order to build up a holistic picture of young people in order to address their needs.

The education of children who are deaf has led to much discussion for more than 200 years, the source of the argument being about whether the emphasis should be on encouraging spoken language, known as the aural/oral method, or whether signing should be seen as a gateway to communication. There are 22 schools for deaf pupils in the UK, including one in Northern Ireland and three in Scotland. Some of the 18 schools in England also accept pupils who have other communication difficulties as well as deafness. The different approaches that are used will depend, at least in part, on the needs of the pupil population. The case study which follows shortly is about a school where children are admitted if their EHC plans state that there is a requirement or preference for British Sign Language (BSL) and/or sign support in order to access the curriculum. Pupils may have other needs as well, but the main need must be their deafness.

British Sign Language (BSL)

Almost 20 years after BSL was recognised as a language, and well after the BSL (Scotland) Act had been passed, in June 2021 a private members' Bill was presented in Parliament by Labour's West Lancashire MP, Rosie Cooper, in order to provide the legal recognition the Deaf community had long sought. In introducing her Bill, she said: *"As the daughter of profoundly deaf parents, BSL is my first language. I know first-hand the difficulty that deaf people face every day. So often they are ignored, misunderstood or have to fight for attention"*. The term used for those who learn to communicate in sign language before learning to speak due to having deaf parents is CODA – Child of Deaf Adults. In a refreshing and unusual display of solidarity, MPs voted unanimously for the Bill to become an Act and in March 2022, the BSL Act was passed. It was a happy coincidence that, during the passage of the Bill, awareness of BSL was heightened by Rose Ayling-Ellis, the first deaf actress and BSL user to take part in the television dance competition, *Strictly Come Dancing*. She went on to win it with her professional partner, Giovanni Pernice. They followed this up by winning the 2022 British Academy Television Awards for the "Must See TV Moment" when the music fell silent during their dance to celebrate the Deaf community and they carried on without missing a beat.

Heathlands School, St Albans, Herts

The next case study is about Heathlands School, which has its own BSL Centre. This was opened in 2009 by Digby, Lord Jones of Birmingham. The Centre offers a range of courses to the general public, local schools, and community groups. Special classes are available every week for the parents of children who are deaf. Heathlands School acts as both a regional and national resource, with over 25 LAs sending pupils to the school.

Case study: Heathlands School, St Albans

Heathlands school has 130 pupils and is on a single site within spacious grounds. The school has two departments: The Lower School (nursery to Year 6) and Upper School (Years 7–11). In order to ensure that the curriculum matches the child, there is some flexibility about where children are placed. All teachers have the additional qualification for teaching deaf pupils and the staff are fluent BSL users. Specialist speech and language therapists assess pupils' needs and deliver tailor made intervention programmes. Running through both departments is an emphasis on communication, language and literacy, as these are seen as the foundation stones for the effective education of Deaf children.

The school's total communication philosophy includes:

- British Sign Language (BSL)
- Sign Supported English (SSE)
- spoken English
- written English
- visual support for teaching, including through Information and Communications Technology (ICT)
- lip-reading
- listening, using hearing aids/implants/radio aids.

This approach allows children to optimise their language skills. In addition, the SaLT Team use a range of strategies and interventions, including:

- LEGO Therapy
- Shape Coding
- Smile Therapy
- Visual Phonics
- Word Aware

Teaching staff embed Shape Coding, Visual Phonics, and Word Aware into daily lessons to support pupils' reading comprehension and the use of spoken and written English. This is important for all pupils and particularly those for whom English is their second language. As well as working closely with the SENCO team and pastoral team, the SaLT team works with other professionals involved with the children, including auditory implant centres, educational audiologists, and Deaf CAMHS.

The residential provision, Heath House, caters for around 20 boarders, and other pupils stay on for an extended day so they can participate in extra-curricular activities. These are designed round the children's interests and have included underwater hockey, football training, swimming clubs, and a youth club for deaf children.

Much of the information on the school's website is in BSL as well as English. Heathlands caters for children who need a total communication approach and is not suitable for those whose needs are met through purely oral/aural methods. The additional intervention strategies used at the school to support the development of language, signed, spoken and written, include the well-established LEGO Therapy. Some information about more recent approaches used by the school are provided in the following Information point.

Information point: Intervention strategies

Shape Coding system Designed by the SaLT Dr Susan Ebbels, this is a visual way of teaching spoken and written grammar, by making grammatical rules visual, using shapes for grammatical structures; colours for part of speech; and arrows for tense and aspect. It is used with any pupils who need visual support to help them understand English grammar. https://shapecoding.com/

smiLE Therapy Developed in 2002 by SaLT Karin Schamroth specifically for children who are BSL users and those who use SSE, this approach is also used more widely with any pupils who need help in developing effective face-to-face communication in everyday situations. The necessary skills are taught explicitly and are broken down into manageable components. https://www.smiletherapytraining.com

Visual Phonics Created by Babs Day, a Teacher of the Deaf (ToD), this gives each sound a visual cue which is signed near the face to encourage lip-reading, but also to indicate where the sound is produced, for example, the nasal sound of "m" uses the same fingers as the letter "m", but is placed on the nose. http://www.visualphonicsbyhand.co.uk/

Word Aware Created after research by Anna Branagan and Stephen Parsons, this is a whole school approach to promoting vocabulary development in a systematic way. This approach uses a STAR approach: **S**elect words from the curriculum; **T**each them in a variety of ways; **A**ctivate the words by using them many times and in different contexts; **R**eview the words to fix them in the long-term memory. This approach has been used both with SEND pupils and those learning English as an additional language. https://www.integratedtreatmentservices.co.uk/our-approaches/speech-therapy-approaches/word-aware/

As mentioned previously in this chapter, one of the consultation questions in the SEND Green Paper recognises the need to encourage more commissioning at regional level. For schools whose pupils are described as "low incidence high cost", and who draw their pupils from a wide range of LAs, this is essential. Co-Head Teacher, Lesley Reeves Costi, adds:

> The importance of having enough children to form a peer group, with children learning alongside their peers rather than in an isolated capacity as deaf children do, cannot be overestimated. At Heathlands their learning experience is similar to a hearing child in mainstream- they are taught directly by a teacher who understands their needs, working and learning alongside peers of the same language and identity. This is why special schools need to be invested in continuously and grown in areas where there is a need.

Moving on from the case studies of two individual schools, the next case study is about a maintained provision which is the first of two specialist MATs.

Orchard Hill College and Academy Trust (OHC&AT)

The composition of OHC&AT will be explained in more detail shortly, but first there is a conversation with Julia James, who is the South West Regional Lead for the Trust and also Principal of Bedelsford School. This is followed by a case study of her school and individual case studies of two of her pupils.

In conversation with Julia James, Principal of Bedelsford School and SW Regional Lead for OHC&AT

Q. Could you explain what made you interested in special education?

A. In my teens, I helped to provide activities at a residential school for children who had cerebral palsy, spina bifida, and other physical disabilities. At one time, I thought of going into paediatric nursing, but instead, I went back to the same school helping on the care side. After that, I worked as a teaching assistant in a behaviour unit before becoming a teaching assistant in a special school. During this time, I started work-based teacher training and later gained a BA (Hons) in Primary Education. My husband worked in social care and when I was in my early twenties, we started providing respite care for children with disabilities.

Q. When did you join Bedelsford School and what made you choose it?

A. I had completed a Post Graduate Diploma in Multi-Sensory Impairment and had a Teaching and Learning Responsibility for Integrated Services with a particular focus on teaching and learning for children with physical and complex disabilities. After gaining experience as a deputy head, I joined Bedelsford School in 2012, which was before it became part of the Trust. Our family includes two adopted children who have cerebral palsy and autism, and I was keen to champion aspirational experiences and outcomes for pupils who have physical and complex needs. I am also interested in how health and social care can work together with education. My schools had been involved in Barry Carpenter's research into children who have complex learning difficulties and disabilities (CLDD) and I was able to look at how integrated therapy teams working with teachers could work in a way that would provide better support for pupils.

Q. In the time you have been there has the pupil population changed much?

A. A major change has been the increase in number of pupils. This has risen from 54 to 125. The number who have sensory or medical needs, such as being oxygen dependent or having rare syndromes has also increased. Due to the number who have been born prematurely and advances in medical care, we have a growing number of pupils who previously may not have survived until school age We look at the main barriers to learning and establish the key skills needed to unlock potential. We have developed three curriculum pathways. There is a pre-formal curriculum to suit those who have very limited cognitive ability; a semi-formal one for those who fall in the middle; and a more formal curriculum for the most able pupils we have. Flexibility is key, as pupils needs change over time and all pathways have fully integrated therapies and medical support.

Q. Could you tell us about the range of therapies you offer?

A. The College and the Academies in the Trust employ their own therapists or partnership with local authorities to provide. The LA where my school is based provides speech and language therapy for pupils at my school who live in the borough and we provide for pupils who come from other LAs. We can explain to everyone working for the Trust what ethos is expected of them, including those who are not directly employed. We aim to work in partnership to foster integrated working with teachers and class teams to support children. While safety is paramount, we aim to overcome any clinical barriers to ensure achievement of aspirational educational needs. We employ our own music therapists, creative art therapists, and communication specialists as well as partnership working with the LA for physiotherapists, occupational therapists, educational psychologist, and a full-time nurse and health team.

Q. Why did you decide to join a MAT and what made you become part of OHC&AT?

A. We had recently opened our 16+ provision and wanted to be able to offer pupils more choice and opportunities. There were other specialist provisions in Kingston who were considering joining Orchard Hill College Academy Trust and we found their ethos matched ours, so in 2016 we became part of the Trust. This also meant we could create secure pathway opportunities for our pupils at the college centres. We were the sixth school to join the Trust and there are now 14 schools. As well as special schools deciding to join us, the DfE can ask the Trust to take on special schools that Ofsted have identified require intervention. We can provide them with a strong family of support.

Q. What do you see as the advantages and disadvantages of being part of a MAT?

A. The advantages far outweigh any disadvantages because you are part of a team who support each other. More special school places and services are needed and we have, for example, been able to work together with LAs to open satellite provisions for Austism Spectrum Disorder and pupils who have pathological demand avoidance (PDA). We want to develop more outreach through being part of the Trust including developing our own mental health service which we can share with others. As to any disadvantages, there are additional layers of regulation which can be frustrating, but the Trust's core purpose and ethos is what matters to the children and the rationale for it.

Q. As you are used to working across the services, have you any advice on how to make a reality of interagency working?

A. Making sure there is a full exchange of information and finding solutions to overcome any clinical barriers are both essential to improve children's outcomes and quality of life. Working together to support students and families from the beginning of their school experience alongside a shared vision and strategy is key. We recently held a conference which brought together therapy, nursing, and education staff from across the Trust and College. This secured a solid foundation and a shared understanding of ethos and vision to lead us into the future.

Q. Is there anything else you would like to add?

A. I support the Green Paper's approach of looking at SEND and alternative provision as one system, but it also needs to iron out the fact that different LAs have different amounts and types of provision. LA boundaries can be problematic for families if a pupil lives the wrong side of a border, even if the most suitable school is nearer than the one in their own LA. For example, additional transport costs can be incurred or may lead to the Special Educational Needs and Disability Tribunal (SENDIST).

Case study: Bedelsford School, Kingston, Surrey

Bedelsford is an Ofsted "Outstanding" school that provides for 125 pupils aged 2–19, who have a wide range of physical disabilities, learning difficulties, and complex health needs. Many of the pupils also have CLDD (complex learning difficulties and disabilities) which means that, in addition to their physical disability, pupils have at least one other coexisting condition such as epilepsy, sensory impairment, or an associated diagnosis of a syndrome such as Down syndrome or Rett syndrome. On average pupils have three coexisting conditions. Exceptionally a child may be admitted for an assessment period pending the completion of their EHCP. This can also happen when a child arrives from overseas, or after hospitalisation following an accident or illness.

Staff aim to empower pupils to overcome their physical challenges and to take an active role in managing their physical and complex needs. They encourage pupils to become more independent and to develop a positive attitude to life. There is an emphasis on enabling pupils to reach their full potential in the key skills of:

- Communication
- Mobility and physical development
- Thinking skills

- Independence skills
- Social and Emotional skills

Parents are automatically members of the Friends of Bedelsford, which is a registered charity organising activities and fundraising events for the school.

Pupils throughout the school access learning opportunities both in indoor and outdoor learning environments. This includes a bespoke hydrotherapy pool, adapted accessible equipment in the playgrounds, Forest School, adventure experiences such as abseiling, and residential opportunities. All class teachers and teams are trained and encouraged to provide safe and exciting learning opportunities and we work closely with our families, therapy, and nursing teams to ensure all children can access opportunities successfully.

The school is keen to take account of the development of neuroscientific knowledge and research to develop the skills of the staff team. Staff are trained to understand the unique way pupils learn and are supported to implement the teaching strategies to ensure pupils make maximum progress. As well as INSET (In-service training) days, there are weekly training sessions and further twilight CPD (continuing professional development) opportunities. These include opportunities for teaching assistants (TAs) to develop their skills, for example TA Apprentices completing level 3 training or gaining healthcare assistant qualifications.

Following the easing of the pandemic, the school plans to develop further its links with mainstream provision and to offer outreach services to schools and colleges. This also supports access by Bedelsford pupils to mainstream settings for those who would benefit.

Our Assistant Head Teacher for Integrated Services, Jessica Webb, has written the following case studies to evidence positive pupil outcomes when integrated working is achieved.

Individual case studies: Two Bedelsford School pupils

Student T is ten years old and has cerebral palsy and complex needs. He had previously been assessed cognitively between 0–11 months and was not ready to use an eye gaze device.

In school, T's teacher worked alongside his SaLT to assess which communication methods might work best for him. He was taught how to use "yes/no" cards to give a consistent response and was taught to use auditory scanning in a PODD (pragmatic, organised, dynamic display) book to access increasingly complex vocabulary. Alongside this, T had regular opportunities to learn the skills of tracking, targeting, and making choices on a school eye gaze device. He engaged with this in 1:1 SaLT sessions and within his learning in the classroom. He was soon able to identify how to greet his peers and use the device in phonics and maths sessions and across his school day. His SaLT spent time training his family so he could use the eye gaze and PODD at home as well.

As he developed his communication skills, T was able to engage further in his learning. He was reassessed to be working within 40–60 month cognitive age bracket. T then was granted a permanent loan from a communication hub. Since receiving this, he has been able to use his aid to speak to his friends, engage in learning, and share his thoughts, excitement and joy with people around him.

Alongside this and in partnership with his physiotherapist, T was given an opportunity to trial a power chair. The physiotherapist provided advice on postural management and the teacher gave opportunities for T to use the power chair in learning through play opportunities and to complete special jobs around the school. As a result of this, he was able to secure a power chair loan from a local hub and continues to develop his skills.

Student J has a diagnosis of Down syndrome, autism spectrum disorder, and chronic lung disease (for which he requires constant oxygen therapy), and global developmental delay (GDD). It became necessary for him to be admitted to hospital for tests under a general anaesthetic. As he had become very distressed by previous hospital visits, his teacher gathered information and resources from the school's nursing and therapy teams and the community and health professionals involved in his care. She continued to work closely with J and his parents to prepare for his next hospital visit.

J's preparation included a hospital passport for his parents to share with hospital staff, containing important medical information and explaining how he communicated using a mixture of vocalisations, gestures, signs, and symbols on his PODD book and a Hi Tech AAC (augmentative and alternative communication) device. The SaLT team produced a social story based on what would happen to him in hospital and this was read to him daily at home and at school. His teacher provided his parent with Makaton training for key signs he would need in hospital. As J enjoyed role play, the teacher provided doctors and nurses uniforms, together with bandages, toy stethoscopes, and a pocket rhesus mask. At first, he was apprehensive with the medical items, but following the intervention and combined with music therapy he later used the items and his PODD to express understanding of what would happen on his hospital visits.

After he was out of hospital and returned to school, J's parent said that all the preparation had meant being in hospital had been much less traumatic for him and his family than on previous occasions.

The final sections on this Trust describe, first of all, its college provision and finally, how the whole Trust, OHC&AT was set up.

Case study: Orchard Hill College

Established in 1983, the college has grown from a small education provision located within a hospital into an Outstanding College with eight centres across London and Surrey. Between them they provide post-16 education for 400 students with a wide range of special educational needs and disabilities.

Each centre is different and has strong links with the community in which they are based and aim to fulfil the vision of building futures and changing lives.

Beaconsfield Centre, New Malden This centre can accommodate up to 55 students and is within walking distance of New Malden town centre. There are many facilities on site for learning as well as partnership and work opportunities within the local community.

Camberwell Road, Camberwell Situated close to the town centre in Camberwell Green, the centre accommodates up to 15 students. Students are supported in work opportunities with many local businesses and partnerships in the local community.

Garratt House, Croydon The centre accommodates up to nine students. Students have many links within the local community including Waddon Leisure Centres, Crystal Palace Football Club, and more.

Lomond House, Camberwell Situated just off Camberwell Green and next to the library in the heart of the town centre with access to many facilities including Camberwell Leisure Centre, Lomond House, can accommodate up to 55 students.

Robin Hood Centre, Sutton This centre can accommodate 30 students and is used as a base for the college's WorkStart and Apprenticeship programmes, as well as a Diploma in Education and Training course. In addition, there is the usual range of work opportunities with local business and community groups.

Vocational Centre, Wandsworth This is co-located with Nightingale Community Academy and can accommodate 15 students. It has access to vocational facilities including an on-site farm, allotments, industry kitchen, mechanical workshop, and hairdressing salon, as well as supported work opportunities in the community.

Vocational Progression Centre, Carshalton The centre can accommodate up to 60 students. The centre has strong links with the community and students regularly access two working allotments.

Park View Centre, Uxbridge The centre accommodates up to 75 students and is near Uxbridge town centre. The centre has a range of on-site vocational opportunities available to students, including catering and digital media.

Case study: Orchard Hill College Academy Trust

Orchard Hill College Academy Trust (OHC&AT) was established in 2013 by Orchard Hill College and has grown into a large special Trust providing for over 1,500 pupils and students, who represent all designations of SEND and range in age from nursery through to sixth form. Together the Trust and the college form Orchard Hill College & Academy Trust.

The Trust is divided into four regional hubs covering London, Surrey, Sussex, and Berkshire. While every one of the schools has something innovative to offer, some of the more recent developments are detailed in the following.

In September 2019, **Dysart School** in Surbiton, which caters for 150 pupils aged 4–19 who have a range of severe and complex needs including autism, worked in partnership with Kingston Council and Tolworth School (which is a federation of an infant and nursery school plus a junior school), to open a satellite provision known as Apollo 1. Two years later, Dysart opened a second satellite site, Apollo 2, adjacent to Latchmere School in the same town. These developments have led to increased opportunities for mainstream integration to the benefit of all the pupils and staff involved.

In addition to its special schools, the Trust has **The Skills Hub** which is a co-educational alternative provision for pupils in the London Borough of Hillingdon. It began by offering 50 places to pupils aged 11–16, many of whom have been, or are at risk of, permanent exclusion. Each student is assigned a skills coach and they are the main point of contact for a student to ensure they are on track and able to achieve. In January 2023, The Skills Hub is due to become a free school and move onto a purpose-built site and expand its intake to 120 pupils aged from 5 to 19.

In September 2020, the first free school to join the Trust was Addington Valley Academy, which opened in temporary buildings in Croydon before moving into a purpose-built school, where it will grow to 150 places for pupils aged 2–19 who have autism, social communication, cognitive, sensory, social, emotional, and behavioural needs.

The Trust is continuing to expand, with three more live free school projects in progress which are due to open between now and 2024.

OHC&AT is satisfied that by using its regional hubs model, it will be able to grow without losing its sense of working in collaborative partnership and ensuring it succeeds in its vision to truly transform lives.

In the SEND Green Paper, there is a question on whether or not specialist MATs should be encouraged. The benefits of being able to draw on the experience and skills of a broader range of staff, employ a wider range of therapists, and have shared training opportunities mean that MATs such as OHC&AT may be able to move forward more easily in terms of intra- and interagency working.

The final case study in this chapter is about Ruskin Mill Trust, which employs practical land and craft activities to support the development of work and life skills with young people with different education needs. Founded by Aonghus Gordon OBE in 1981, the Trust draws inspiration from the work of Rudolf Steiner, John Ruskin, and William Morris and contemporary research.

Case study: Ruskin Mill Trust

Ruskin Mill Trust (RMT) is a charitable Trust whose provisions across England, Wales, and Scotland include

- five colleges for young adults aged 16–25
- four schools for pupils aged 6–19
- two adult social care provisions for adults aged 18 and above

The Trust serves children, young people, and adults with a wide range of different educational needs, autism, and behavioural issues whose needs cannot be met by mainstream establishments.

Pupils at the specialist schools do much of their learning outside the classroom, embedding the requirements of the national curriculum in practical activities such as growing and preparing their own food, caring for animals, craft activities with wool, wood, clay, or metal, and music and drama.

The Trust's colleges support students to overcome barriers to learning and to develop the self-confidence that comes from being able to achieve physical results in challenging circumstances, such as the heat of a forge or glass workshop, or outdoors work in winter (urban-based colleges have farming spaces nearby). As they develop practical skills, they also come to engage with the community, making items that can be used at home, given as gifts, or used in social enterprise, or growing, preparing, and serving food. Many move on to further education, find jobs, or become volunteer workers.

Aonghus Gordon trained as a potter. He gradually developed Ruskin Mill Trust's approach of *Practical Skills Therapeutic Education* (PSTE) in response to the needs of the young people he worked with as it became clear that craft and farming brought about transformations that classroom-based education could not. The physical skills required of a particular craft or farming activity (hands) point towards an overall intellectual grasp of the process of making, growing, cooking, and so on (head), and lead students to encounter and overcome their own barriers to development (heart).

Working with skilled therapeutic educators in a contemporary apprenticeship model, students engage with the given qualities of a particular material across its lifespan (for example: caring for sheep; shearing, carding, spinning, and dyeing wool; working with fleece to make slippers to wear), in a seed-to-table curriculum emphasising connection and transformation over time.

The method of PSTE includes seven fields of practice to provide a rounded and integrated educational experience:

1. Genius Loci (spirit of place): each of RMT's educational centres works holistically with the landscape – its geology, flora and fauna, and history of human activities – to develop a curriculum grounded in locality.
2. Practical Skills: developing craft and practical skills supports physical, cognitive, and emotional development and embeds functional skills. Students source local materials and work them with their own hands to create items of service – food, clothing, utensils, and more.
3. Biodynamic Ecology: the seed-to-table curriculum helps students engage with the rhythms of the seasons while they come to understand the farm as a whole interconnected organism existing in a wider context.
4. Therapeutic Education: the overall pedagogical framework for these activities involves an understanding of human development and applied sensory integration. Age-appropriate activities help students re-step missed developmental opportunities.
5. Holistic Support and Care: RMT seeks to offer a 24-hour educational curriculum, especially in its residential settings where students master basic skills for living, in turn supporting healthy life processes such as nutrition.
6. Holistic Medicine: a multi-disciplinary team of practitioners offers a range of therapies as needed to support students' health and development.
7. Transformative Leadership: acknowledging multiple intelligences, staff consciously role model positive relationships with other people as well as their environment.

Student progress towards independence can be measured in three stages: (1) overcoming barriers to learning; (2) becoming skilled; (3) contributing to the wider community. Each of these stages demonstrates the student ability for self-generated conscious action.

The Trust invests heavily in staff training and offers courses externally, including a master's degree in practical skills therapeutic education. Senior staff are seconded to carry out PhDs in relevant academic disciplines and the Trust has a substantial internal research effort (see https://www.thefieldcentre.org.uk/).

Aonghus Gordon's long history of restoring redundant iconic industrial buildings and transforming them into educational and cultural centres was recognised in the award of an OBE for services to heritage and education.

While not every school or college will be able to provide activities that depend on having spacious grounds or being near the countryside, some of the ideas contained in this Trust's approach, including the need to find ways of engaging pupils' interest through learning beyond the walls of the classroom and offering opportunities for more time spent in being active and having practical tasks, whether inside or outdoors, is worth exploring further.

Conclusions

This chapter and the previous one has tried to show what is needed in order to ensure that all children can be included somewhere along a continuum of provision. Although the majority of pupils have always been in mainstream provision, more could join them if there were sufficient support available to schools. However, even if that were forthcoming, there will always be children who cannot cope with the hustle and bustle of a busy school and who need a different environment in order to thrive, and not just survive, their years of schooling. There is nothing wrong with accepting that what is provided for the majority will not suit a minority and that minority is made larger by the pressure on today's children of constant testing, in trying to push them up to "expected standards", and getting them through the English Baccalaureate (EBacc), whether or not that will motivate them to become lifelong learners.

References

British Sign Language (BSL) Act 2022. Available from https://www.gov.uk/government/publications/british-sign-language-bill-and-explanatory-notes-bsl-version

BSL (Scotland) Act 2015. Available from https://www.legislation.gov.uk/asp/2015/11/contents/enacted

Gov.Uk (2015) *SEND Code of Practice: 0 to 25 Years.* Available from https://www.gov.uk/government/publications/send-code-of-practice-0-to-25

Gov.UK (2017) *Transforming Children and Young People's Mental Health Provision: A Green Paper.* Available from https://www.gov.uk/government/consultations/transforming-children-and-young-peoples-mental-health-provision-a-green-paper

Gov.Uk (2022a) *Levelling Up the United Kingdom.* Available from https://www.gov.uk/government/publications/levelling-up-the-united-kingdom

Gov.UK (2022b) *Opportunity for All: Strong Schools with Great Teachers for Your Child.* Available from https://www.gov.uk/government/publications/opportunity-for-all-strong-schools-with-great-teachers-for-your-child

Gov.UK (2022c) *SEND Review: Right Support, Right Place, Right Time.* Available from https://www.gov.uk/government/consultations/send-review-right-support-right-place-right-time

Gov.Uk (2022d) *Transforming Children and Young People's Mental Health Provision. Implementation Programme.* Available from https://assets.publishing.service.gov.uk/government/uploads/system/uploads/attachment_data/file/1074420/220510_CYPMH_Transparency_Pub.pdf

https://www.integratedtreatmentservices.co.uk/our-approaches/speech-therapy-approaches/colourful-semantics-2/

https://shapecoding.com

https://www.smiletherapytraining.com

https://www.talk4writing.com/

https://www.talk4writing.com/about/

https://www.thefieldcentre.org.uk/

http://www.visualphonicsbyhand.co.uk/

Tutt, R. (2016) *Rona Tutt's Guide to SEND and Inclusion.* London: Sage.

Tutt, R., and Williams, P. (2021) *How to Maximise Emotional Wellbeing and Improve Mental Health.* London and New York: Routledge.

7 Responsibility, Accountability, and Funding

Public services are caught in a cycle of increasing demand and late intervention. Whether in mental health services, the SEND system or children's social care, spending is becoming ever more concentrated on the most complex and expensive interventions. This means less resource for preventive work and fewer early intervention services, leading to further escalation of needs and increased cost.

NCB, 2021 (Build Back Childhood, P7)

This penultimate chapter gives a brief account of funding in education, health, and social care, and how this sits with responsibility and accountability. The focus is first on education funding and how this has changed since Local Management of Schools (LMS) in 1998 gave schools their own budgets. In the case of health and children's social care, the point is made that Directors of Children's Services (DCSs) receive money which is not ring-fenced, so how it is spent will vary in different local authorities (LAs). After this, there are some comments on how people are held to account for the responsibilities they undertake, whether or not the funding is there. The chapter ends with a conversation with Nick Whittaker, a former His Majesty's Inspector (HMI), who describes how he helped to set up a charity to give every young person, regardless of the severity of their needs, the chance to experience climbing, sometimes in the face of overwhelming odds.

Funding for education

All state-funded schools, whether they are academies or council-run schools, get their funding from the government. This is allocated through a National Funding Formula (NFF). In the case of maintained schools, it comes via LAs, whereas for academies it comes from government via the Education and Skills Funding Agency (ESFA). The money LAs receive in order to fund schools and colleges is called the Dedicated Schools Grant (DSG). In addition, mainstream schools can receive "top-up" funding for pupils with a high level of need. This is decided by the Schools Forum.

DOI: 10.4324/9781003333203-10

Information point: Schools Forum

If an LA has any of these schools, they must be represented:

- Primary, secondary, special, and nursery schools
- Pupil referral units (PRUs) and alternative provision (AP) academies
- 16–19 providers
- Early years private, voluntary, and independent (PVI) providers

Most of the Forum's role is consultative. However, decision-making powers include:

- Arrangements for the education of pupils with SEND and the use of PRUs
- The education of children otherwise than at school
- The arrangements for paying top-up funding

At present, unlike mainstream schools, specialist provision, including mainstream schools with specialist units or resourced provision, are funded for each place they provide. This means that they receive a minimum of £10,000 per pupil, with some places costing more depending on the complexity of the child's needs.

Although the block grant is the main funding source for schools, they receive money from other sources as well. Recently, there has been a two-staged consultation on sending money directly to schools instead of via the LA. The response to the first part of the consultation, which ran from July to September 2021, resulted in this approach being agreed. The second one ran from June 2022 to September 2022 and considered how a "direct" NFF might be implemented. It mentions the SEND Green Paper and the need to achieve a more financially sustainable SEND system, with the suggestion that detailed proposals on how high needs funding would operate, might wait for the Green Paper response to be published. For several years there has been pupil premium funding to provide additional funding for pupils who are eligible. The amount of funding changes regularly and the current situation is given in the following:

Information point: Pupil premium

Introduced in 2011 with the aim of reducing the attainment gap for pupils from disadvantaged backgrounds or who have been taken into care or adopted from care. Currently the grant covers:

- Pupils eligible for free school meals (FSM)
- Pupils who have been eligible for FSM during the past six years

- Pupils adopted from care or who have left care
- Pupils from service families (SPP)
- Children of ex-service personnel
- Children looked after by the LA, that is, LAC.

The amount varies each year and is higher for primary than secondary pupils on FSM, but the same for all ages if adopted or LAC. Pupils on FSM are paid at a lower rate than adopted or LAC pupils. The money goes directly to schools, apart from those in the care of the LA, where it goes to the LA. If pupils are eligible for both SPP and pupil premium, the school is entitled to apply for both.

By 31st December every year, schools must produce a "Pupil premium strategy statement" using the DfE template.

https://www.gov.uk/government/publications/pupil-premium

Another source of more recent funding, although it is uncertain how much longer it might last, is the National Tutoring Programme which was provided by the government in the wake of the pandemic.

National tutoring programme (NTP)

To help mitigate the impact of the pandemic on pupils whose learning was most affected by it, in the academic year 2020/21, the Department for Education (DfE) introduced a National Tutoring Programme (NTP). In February 2021, Sir Kevan Collins was announced as the government's Education Recovery Commissioner. By June that year he had resigned, saying the money the government was putting aside did not match up to the amount that was needed to help pupils recover from the time in school they had missed during the pandemic. The government later raised the amount but nothing near to the total Sir Kevan said was necessary. Sir Kevan was not replaced. In its second year, the NTP was delivered by the Dutch multinational service provider, Randstad. When it failed to reach the anticipated number of pupils, the government agreed to send the money directly to schools to arrange their own provision. For the year 2022 to 2023, the DfE set out three routes providing subsidised tuition in its update guidance published in October 2022.

Extra funding for LAs

In recognition of the fact that many LAs were having difficulty controlling their high needs systems, from 2020–21 the DfE introduced two programmes offering direct support:

- The Safety Valve programme for LAs with the highest deficits
- The Delivering Better Value (DBV) in SEND programme for a further 55 LAs with what are referred to as "less severe but substantial deficits"

In setting out guidance for LAs on "Sustainable high needs systems", the DfE clarified that one source of difficulty is that the high needs budget is sometimes used for health and/or social care provision and that the DSG must only be used to fund educational provision:

> It is essential that LAs work with health and social care partners in sharing responsibility of specialist provision for children and young people. Health partners have statutory responsibilities to secure and fund the health provision specified in EHCPs. Through the Safety Valve programme, we have seen that this is not always happening in practice to a sufficient level. Many LAs have been using their high needs budget to fund provision or resources that come under the remit of health or social care.
>
> (2022c: 15)

The state of school funding

In 2021, the view of school leaders was that they were under increasing pressure from lack of funds. At a parliamentary launch of a report into school funding by the National Association of Head Teachers (NAHT), Paul Whiteman, general secretary of the NAHT, commented:

> The government's failure to invest in schools over the past decade is forcing them to cut back on staff, support for pupils, and activities that enrich the school day. Despite all the rhetoric on additional investment in schools, it is clear that school budgets remain under enormous pressure.
>
> (08.09.21)

This viewpoint coincides with that of the Institute for Fiscal Studies (IFS), who, in August 2022, published a report showing that by 2024 school funding will be 3% below levels in 2010 in real terms. This is in contrast to the government talking about the Schools Bill as being *"backed by huge government investment – core school funding will rise by £4 billion in 2022/23 compared with 2021/22, which represents a 7% increase per pupil.*

Funding for health and social care

The Department of Health and Social Care (DHSC) provides money to the NHS and to LAs for social care. The DHSC sets out what the NHS is expected to deliver for the funding it receives. NHS England passes on most of the money to its integrated care systems (ICSs). These were given legal status through the Health and Care Act 2022, which was discussed in Chapter 4 of this book. In the same way that money is apportioned to schools through a formula, there is a formula for deciding how much each ICS will receive. This depends partly on the size of the local population, the age profile, health status, and level of deprivation. In addition, the formula considers the different costs of staff, buildings, and the delivery of services in different parts of the country.

Children and young people are named in the Health and Care Act as requiring specific consideration. This means that meeting children's health and care needs is at the centre of integrated care boards' (ICBs) responsibilities. For children and young people, these services are meant to be delivered in ways which are preventative, reactive, and supportive. They take place in a variety of settings, such as schools, colleges, nursing services, GP surgeries, clinics, children's centres, and family hubs. Between them, they are expected to offer support in trying to give every child the best start in life.

Funding for children's social care

In addition to funding the LA receives from the DHSC, additional money comes from local taxes. Although as explained in the Introductory chapter, responsibility for both education and children's care was placed under one director, increasingly LAs have found that it sometimes makes more sense not to separate children and adult social care services. The funding the DCS receives from government for education and social care is not ring-fenced, so how it is spent will vary between different LAs.

The Local Government Association has warned the government that far more money is needed for children's social care in order to keep up with increasing demand. This includes a significant rise in the number of children taken into care in recent years.

Chapter 3 of this book focused on the review of children's social care. The review reported that the government needed to commit to a five-year programme of reform costing £2.6 billion, due to the extreme stress the system was under. It was envisaged that this sum as being split over four years. In addition, a further £50 million would be needed for other interventions over the investment period. The review also said that the government needed to update the funding formula for children's social care, so that resources were directed to where they were most needed.

Responsibility and accountability

Responsibility and accountability are often considered to be synonymous and used interchangeably. However, responsibility usually refers to someone's duty to carry out certain actions and see them to completion, whereas accountability generally refers to what happens after the action or actions have been completed and someone is held to account for the outcome. As far as education and children's social care are concerned, Ofsted and the Care Quality Commission (CQC) are the dominant factor in holding the services to account. Ofsted and CQC also hold some sway over health in terms of local Area SEND inspections.

Ofsted and schools

Ofsted came into being in 1990 and after 30 years, few people remember that the acronym stands for Office for Standards in Education. Previously, schools had been inspected by HMIs but, unlike now, they were not part of Ofsted and their visits to schools were far and few between.

Today, Ofsted has around 1,800 employees across its eight regions and is responsible for inspecting education, children's services and skills. This includes

- Maintained schools and academies, some independent schools, colleges, apprenticeship providers, prison education, and many other educational institutions and programmes outside of higher education
- Childcare, LAs, adoption and fostering agencies, initial teacher training, and teacher development.

Since 2017, Ofsted has also inspected those on the Register of Apprenticeship Training Providers (RoAPT). Independent schools also have their own inspection service, the Independent Schools Inspectorate (ISI).

Christine Gilbert

In 2012, shortly after she stood down from being Her Majesty's Chief Inspector (HMCI), Christine Gilbert wrote an article for the National College for School Leadership (NCSL) suggesting that, although she saw Ofsted as having an ongoing role, there needed to be more emphasis on schools being accountable for their own improvement:

> The public accountability regime established by the 1988 Education Reform Act challenged the view that professionals alone could be trusted to deliver high standards and good-quality education. That regime has been a key driver for reform and few would argue for a return to a self-defining and self-regulating professionalism. However, 30 years on, with a self-improving system well under way, it is time to re-balance the current framework by giving greater emphasis to school-led accountability that is rooted in moral purpose and professionalism.
>
> (2012: 23)

Since then, the self-evaluation form (SEF), although no longer compulsory, sits alongside the school development plan (SDP) and inspectors usually take an active interest in both these documents.

In 2018, the DfE published a policy paper, which indicated that school accountability had become too heavy and they would reduce it:

> At present, school leaders can feel accountable to multiple masters, with different demands placed on them. We will remove duplication and be clear which actor – Ofsted; the Department for Education through Regional School Commissioners (RSCs); local authorities; MATs; and schools themselves – is playing which distinct role.
>
> (2018: 1)

In the same year as the DfE's policy paper, the NAHT published the results of its commission on accountability. This reached a different conclusion on how the undoubted pressure and workload caused by an Ofsted inspector's visit could be substantially reduced:

> Ofsted continues to perform a critical function by identifying failure in the system so that no child attends a poor school. Yet the accountability system provides little benefit to the pupils, parents and staff at the vast majority of schools in this country that are not failing. At best it is a distraction on the journey from good to great. At worst it works against improvement by incentivising the wrong actions and behaviours. At a system level, the approaches used by the government to hold schools to account are acting as a brake to overall improvement.
>
> (2018: 4)

Local area SEND inspections

Ofsted and CQC have carried out joint inspections of every local area in the last five years. The inspections were about how far the SEND reforms of 2014 had been embedded. A new framework started in 2023 and will focus more on the experience of children who have SEND and their families, rather than holding meetings with the leaders in the area.

Inspection of LA children's services

The system of inspections for LA children's services is known as ILACS (inspecting local authority children's services). These inspections focus on the effectiveness of the LA's arrangements and services. There is no fixed cycle of inspections, which may involve a standard or short inspection, or a focused visit. Inspections include a graded judgement and a focused visit may be one of the outcomes. Focused visits are also used when an inspection is not due and is seen as an opportunity to identify what is going well and what needs to improve before the next inspection.

Joint targeted area inspections

These inspections are carried out by inspectors from:

- Ofsted
- The Care Quality Commission (CQC)
- His Majesty's Inspectorate of Constabulary and Fire & Rescue Service

The inspections focus on the multi-agency arrangements for children and families who need help. New guidance came out in October 2022 for those carrying out these inspections.

To end this chapter, there is a conversation with Nick Whittaker, a former HMI, about the charity he helped to establish. Charities have been having a tough time in recent years, partly as the result of the pandemic and partly due to people in general having less cash to spare.

Until a year ago, Nick Whittaker was working for Ofsted as an HMI and Specialist Adviser for SEND. Along with his day job, he was involved in the charity he helped to found, Climbing for All Sheffield. Before the conversation with Nick, here is some information about his charity and where it is based.

Information point: Climbing for All Sheffield

Climbing for All Sheffield (CfAS) was founded in 2016 to help children, young people, and adults with a range of disabilities enjoy climbing and being a part of the climbing community. However, its story started in 2013 when Clare, a 14-year-old girl with complex difficulties caused by a stroke, was determined to climb. There is a film about Clare and the origins of CfAS called *Reach: a teenage climber defines her own limits*, available at
https://www.youtube.com/watch?v=JiTDrjru52s.

Clare was introduced to the Whittaker family, and on finding there were other differently abled young people who wanted to give climbing a go, Nick and his children, Ruby, Robin, and Hazel, together with Clare and her mum, Jenny, decided to set up the charity. CfAS is based at the Foundry Climbing Centre in Sheffield, which is one of the hubs for indoor climbing in the UK, equipped for climbers at all levels from beginners up to elite-level competition climbers.

Climbing instructors, volunteers and supporters have kept CfAS going, and although affected by the pandemic, the charity has continued to grow. Annual fundraising events are held so that climbing is subsidised with a "pay as you feel" approach, so no one is excluded because of cost. The charity runs on the kindness and generosity of everyone involved, especially the Foundry Climbing Centre and the team of volunteer climbers who make climbing fun and accessible for a wide range of children, young people and adults.

In conversation with Nick Whittaker, founder of the charity, Climbing for All Sheffield (CfAS)

Q. Tell us about your charity and how you make climbing accessible and inclusive.

A. It took a long time to get the charity going, but we've tapped into a huge amount of generosity and a deep seam of kindness in the climbing community. This exemplifies the culture of climbing, which is all about looking out for one another.

The centre we use is the Foundry Climbing Centre in Sheffield, so we start by following all their safety protocols. We've developed additional safety systems and guidance because we're helping vulnerable people to participate in activities that wouldn't normally be accessible. This might mean using a specialised harness and a pulley system for someone who has limited mobility or creating social stories so that someone knows what is going to happen in a climbing session and understands how to keep safe and enjoy climbing. Beyond this, taking decisions about risks is never easy. One young person with complex physical and health needs said to us during the pandemic: *"Look, I'm ill and I'm not going to get better. I may not be able to do this for long, so as far as I'm concerned, what climbing does for both my physical and mental health far outweighs any risks."* To help to make climbing more inclusive, we have delivered training to climbing instructors both at our own centre and at other climbing centres in Sheffield. Recently, we had visitors from six European countries who came to see what we're doing and to learn how they might increase participation in outdoor and adventurous activities in their own countries.

Now we're fully up and running again after Covid and we're hoping to have some third year medical students from the University of Sheffield with us for a month. We want to ask them to gather views from the climbers and the volunteers about their experiences. By listening to what they say and collecting data, we hope we can understand more about why fewer children and young people who have learning difficulties and disabilities, physical difficulties, and social communication difficulties, including autism, participate in climbing and other adventure sports.

Q. How do you find working across the services?

A. Our volunteers include a range of health professionals who are climbers themselves and are really interested in inclusive climbing. They say that there is strong evidence for the therapeutic value of climbing, as it's a motivating activity that develops people's strength, co-ordination, balance, and movement. It also supports the development of people's language and communication and has huge benefits for their confidence and self-image as well as their wider physical and emotional health. Many of our young people overcome profound difficulties associated with their physical health or disability when they climb. For some, it has been the thing that has re-energised them, giving them a stronger and more positive view of themselves, and for others it has opened the door to things that they didn't think were going to be possible!

We know that occupational therapy (OT) practice is all about how to make the inaccessible accessible and that is what we're trying to do. We've used the knowledge and experience of climbers and friends to find solutions to the problems people experience and, when needed, we've tapped into expert help from therapists and others such as clinical scientists. We always think about what the problem is and how it might be overcome. We try to do this in a person-centred way by really listening to our climbers, thinking about what is important to them, and working out how best to support them, One of our volunteers is a specialist teacher of children with multi-sensory impairment (MSI). His vast knowledge of how to support children and young people [and adults] who have significant sensory impairments has been invaluable.

This has meant that we have been able to introduce some of our climbers to climbing in the Peak District.

Climbing relies on communication and we've had really good help and advice from speech and language therapists about inclusive communication and using different methods of augmentative communication such as pictures, symbols, and signs.

In terms of social care, we have some young people where either they or their family have chosen climbing as one of the main activities of their week and they come with their personal assistant (PA). We think this is really helping those young people to be more visible in the community as well as participating in a great physically based activity. Some parents have told us that it's hard to find activities in the evenings or at the weekend where the family feels welcome and their children can be fully included. We've worked hard to make them feel welcome and included in climbing! We've also had some young people who are in care or who are moving into independent living, so we try to provide inclusive opportunities for them and help them to feel less socially isolated.

Q. Are you seen as a form of alternative provision (AP) or social prescribing?

A. We don't really fall into a category. We're just a group of people with an interest in climbing who want to make it more accessible, because we can see the benefits it brings. Sometimes it takes time. For example, it took several weeks for one young person to "find his feet". His teachers thought he might enjoy climbing so we gave it a go! On his first visit, he refused to get out of the minibus. On the next two visits, he got off the minibus and lay down in the car park. Eventually, he came inside but refused to put on a climbing harness. But once we did manage to get him into it and he started climbing, he was absolutely gripped. He is still climbing nearly five years later! We've made some simple adjustments such as making groups smaller and, for those who like it quieter, we'll give them an earlier session when there are fewer people about. Sometimes I climb with a young person who is a total livewire, which makes it unsafe when others are climbing, so we climb together when the centre is almost empty [early on weekday mornings]. My aim is to get to the point that he can climb safely when the centre is busier but I know it will take time.

Q. What do you think of the SEND Green Paper?

A. I'm concerned that the proposals focus too much on top-down accountability and the creation of a new regulatory framework. It's absolutely right that there are legal and contractual obligations, but the importance of networks and partnerships should be more prominent in SEND accountability, especially in the forms of accountability that carry 'high-stakes' consequences!

I am worried that the education system and wider SEND system has become more atomised in recent years and that the construct of inclusion that now dominates in these systems lacks real meaning and ambition for children, young people, and families. I see this as a much wider public policy problem.

The goals of the most significant reforms in my professional life, such as the Valuing People White Paper, are yet to be realised and the picture painted by the Lamb Enquiry is as observable now as it was more than ten years ago. Despite this, I am optimistic because I can see how individuals and groups, such as those in the climbing community, want to be inclusive and are willing to put time and energy into making it happen!

Some of the themes Nick raises are taken up in the next chapter.

Conclusions

There is a complex web of connections between responsibility, accountability, and funding. Should people be held to account if, rather than offering to take on a responsibility, they have been told to do so and then find they cannot do everything expected of them, or do what is required to the right standard? Is it reasonable for people to be accountable for something over which they have limited control? And what happens if the resources simply are not there to support what they are trying to achieve? When funding across the services is so tight that these situations can and do arise, holding people to account for their actions should be weighed against the obstacles that stood in the way of what they might have achieved.

References

Gilbert, C. (2012) *Towards a Self-Improving System: The Role of School Accountability*. Available from https://dera.ioe.ac.uk/14919/1/towards-a-self-improving-system-school-accountability-thinkpiece%5B1%5D.pdf

DfE (2018) *Policy Paper Principles for a Clear and Simple School Accountability System*. Available from https://www.gov.uk/government/publications/principles-for-a-clear-and-simple-school-accountability-system

DfE (2021a) *Fair school funding for all: completing our reforms to the National Funding Formula Government consultation*. Available from https://consult.education.gov.uk/funding-policy-unit/completing-our-reforms-to-the-nff/supporting_documents/Fair%20Funding%20For%20All%20Consultation.pdf

DfE (2021b) *Review of National Funding Formula for Allocations of High Needs Funding to Local Authorities: Changes for 2022–23 – Consultation*. Available from https://consult.education.gov.uk/funding-policy-unit/high-needs-nff-proposedchanges/supporting_documents/High%20needs%20NFF%20review%20consultation%20document.pdf

DfE (2022a) *Guidance on our intervention work with local authorities*. https://assets.publishing.service.gov.uk/government/uploads/system/uploads/attachment_data/file/1110657/Sustainable_high_needs_systems_guide_-_SV_and_DBV_updates_-_Oct22.pdf

DfE (2022b) *Implementing the Direct National Funding Formula Government consultation*. Available from https://consult.education.gov.uk/funding-policy-unit/implementing-the-direct-national-funding-formula/supporting_documents/Implementing%20the%20direct%20national%20funding%20formula%20%20government%20consultation.pdf

DfE (2022c) *Sustainability in High Needs Systems Guidance for Local Authorities*. Available from https://assets.publishing.service.gov.uk/government/uploads/system/uploads/attachment_data/file/1084835/Local_authority_guidance_on_high_needs_sustainability.pdf

DoH (2001) *Valuing People – A New Strategy for Learning Disability for the 21st Century*. Available from: https://assets.publishing.service.gov.uk/government/uploads/system/uploads/attachment_data/file/250877/5086.pdf

ESFA (2021) *Schools Forum Operational and Good Practice Guide*. Available from https://assets.publishing.service.gov.uk/government/uploads/system/uploads/attachment_data/file/971710/Schools_forum_operational_and_good_practice_guide_amended_March_2021.pdf

Gov.Uk (1988) *Education Reform Act*. Available from https://www.legislation.gov.uk/ukpga/1988/40/contents

Gov.UK (2002) *Education Act*. Available from https://www.legislation.gov.uk/ukpga/2002/32/contents

Gov, UK (2009) *Lamb Inquiry: Special Educational Needs and Parental Confidence*. Available from: http://www.specialeducationalneeds.co.uk/uploads/1/1/4/6/11463509/lamb_inquiry

Gov.Uk (2022a) *Health and Care Act*. Available from https://www.legislation.gov.uk/ukpga/2022/31/contents/enacted

Gov.UK (2022) *National Tutoring Programme*. Available from https://www.gov.uk/government/publications/national-tutoring-programme-guidance-for-schools-2022-to-2023

Gov.Uk (2022c) *Joint Targeted Area Inspection of the Multi-Agency Response to Children and Families Who Need Help*. Available from https://www.gov.uk/government/publications/joint-targeted-area-inspection-of-the-multi-agency-response-to-children-and-families-who-need-help/joint-targeted-area-inspection-of-the-multi-agency-response-to-children-and-families-who-need-help

Gov.Uk (2022d) *Pupil Premium: Overview*. Available from https://www.gov.uk/government/publications/pupil-premium/pupil-premium

Gov.Uk (2022e) *Schools Bill*. Available from https://www.gov.uk/government/news/new-schools-bill-to-boost-education-standards-across-the-country

Gov.Uk (2022f) *SEND Review: Right Support, Right Place, Right Time*. Available from https://www.gov.uk/government/consultations/send-review-right-support-right-place-right-time

Institute of Fiscal Studies (2022) *School Spending and Costs: The Coming Crunch*. Available from https://ifs.org.uk/publications/school-spending-and-costs-coming-crunch

Local Government Association (2022) *Independent Review of Children's Social Care – LGA Initial View, May 2022*. Available from https://www.local.gov.uk/parliament/briefings-and-responses/independent-review-childrens-social-care-lga-initial-view-may

MacAlister, J. (2022) *Independent Review of Children's Social Care*. Available from https://childrenssocialcare.independent-review.uk/final-report/

National Childrens Bureau (2021) *Build Back Childhood Campaign*. Available from https://councilfordisabledchildren.org.uk/about-us/media-centre/news-opinion/rishi-sunaks-promise-new-direction-children-and-families

NAHT (2018) *Improving School Accountability: A Report of the NAHT Accountability Commission*. Available from https://www.naht.org.uk/Portals/0/PDF%27s/Improving%20school%20accountability.pdf?ver=2021-04-27-121950-093/

NAHT (2021) *A Failure to Invest – The State of School Funding 2021*. Available from https://www.naht.org.uk/Our-Priorities/Funding/ArtMID/724/ArticleID/1223/A-failure-to-invest-the-state-of-school-funding-2021

Ofsted (2022) *Guidance Joint Targeted Area Inspection of the Multi Agency Response to Children and Families Who Need Help*. Available from https://www.gov.uk/government/publications/joint-targeted-area-inspection-of-the-multi-agency-response-to-children-and-families-who-need-help/joint-targeted-area-inspection-of-the-multi-agency-response-to-children-and-families-who-need-help

8 Conclusion

Achieving better outcomes for all

> This is not a group of children and young people who are ignored by Government programmes and priorities. The challenge is that everybody's business becomes no-one's priority. These children need to become our children.
>
> (Lenehan Review 2017: paragraph 12)

The use of the word "all" in the title of this chapter is deliberate. It encompasses all those who work with children, young people and their families. It includes parents, carers, and the wider family and, of course, the children and young people themselves. At a time when there is a cost of living crisis, the threat of wars escalating, and gathering concern about the impact of climate change on the planet, it may be difficult to be optimistic about the future. While it is true that this may not be the right time for carefree, blue-skies thinking, it is still possible be positive about what could be achieved within the constraints that exist.

This book was written mainly during 2022, when it was clear that there was going to be an unusual opportunity to achieve closer working between education, health, and social care, due to all three services seeking to improve their ways of working. Although Josh MacAlister, at the start of the final report of his review, referred to this as a "*Once in a lifetime opportunity to reset children's social care*", a similar sentiment might apply equally well to the SEND (Special Educational Needs and Disability) Green Paper and the Health and Care Act, with all three developments appearing over three months in the spring and summer of 2022.

This final chapter does not attempt to sum up everything that has come out of the preceding chapters, but to focus instead on some of the broader issues that have emerged and how they might help to point the way forward. These are being encapsulated in the words communication, collaboration, and co-location. They are placed in this order because communication so often seems to lie at the core of everything. It can take many forms, but whatever form it takes, it is essential for building relationships. Once these have been established, it becomes easier to collaborate. These collaborations involve the services of education, health, and social care making sure the various parts of their separate organisations are well co-ordinated internally, as well as strengthening the ties between them. Beyond this, and as the information and examples in this book have shown, there is a range of other partnerships that contribute to improving the lives of children and their families.

DOI: 10.4324/9781003333203-11

While the importance of communication and collaboration will be common to many fields of endeavour, the merits of co-location are particularly pertinent in the current context. One of the ways of making it easier to communicate and to collaborate is to extend the opportunities for co-location. This is considered, both in terms of different provisions within a service physically being placed together, and in opening up opportunities for closer interagency working. Under these three headings, the following paragraphs look at some of the problems that have been identified and how they might be resolved.

Communication

1. Parents and children do not feel they are listened to and their voices count.
2. Children's behaviour may not be recognised as a form of communication.
3. Professionals working in the services do not get the sense that they are valued.

Taking each of these points in turn, there is no doubt that progress has been made in trying to ensure that parents and children are more involved in the decisions that affect them. In 2014, the NHS Five Year Forward View talked about the need for health professionals to have a more equal partnership, rather than telling patients what they should do. In the same year, the Care Act (2014a) stressed the importance of co-production, as a means of consulting the people who use the service and finding solutions together. The Children and Families Act (2014b), as well as clarifying the involvement of all three services in the switch from "statements" to education, health and care plans (EHCPs), emphasised that EHCPs should be co-produced with children and their families. The legislation may be there, but it is up to the people concerned to make it happen and much has already been achieved. It is seen in the way that many medical practitioners engage with their patients; in how social care staff try to work with families in finding solutions together; and how those working in schools and LAs may go out of their way to involve children and families in the decisions that affect them. This way of working could be summed up by the well-known phrase, "Nothing about us without us".

Moving on to the need to recognise that, where there are concerns about a child's behaviour, it should be seen as a form of communication and there may be underlying reasons, whether medical, social, or educational, for the way they are behaving. As explained previously, there is a link here, both with attendance and with exclusion. Primary aged pupils are more likely to attend if they are not made anxious by a curriculum driven by a regime of testing and reaching age-related expectations. They are also more likely to behave in an acceptable manner and not get excluded if they enjoy the range of educational experiences on offer and feel included in them. At secondary level, anxieties or dissatisfaction can occur as a result of a strong focus on achieving enough GCSEs, whether or not this is the right course for them. This is not to blame schools who often go out of their way to allow for pupils' abilities and interests, but to highlight the dangers inherent in the current system of education.

The third point is very much connected to the first, as people of all ages need to feel that they are listened to and their voices can influence what happens, both to them in their individual roles and in helping to effect improvement in the service they work for. The problems of recruitment in all three services and with retaining staff once they have trained is leading to shortages, which can then put more pressure on the remaining staff who have to take on additional responsibilities. Regulating workloads and caseloads is critical in keeping staff and enabling them to continue in posts which by their very nature involve a certain amount of stress and less time to look out for each other. Counselling for both pupils and staff should be available as part of a focus on wellbeing, as well as the need for staff in education to have access to supervision from a trained professional in order to talk over issues that can arise when dealing with pupils or staff who have mental health issues.

Collaboration

1. Intra-agency and interagency working is patchy.
2. Trying to fit the child and family into an existing system rather than the other way round.
3. Widening the definition of partnership working in relation to schools.

Given the size and complexity of the education, health, and social care services, it may not be surprising that there is a need to think in terms of how much joining up there is within each service, as well as encouraging closer multi-professional working across the services. There have been examples in this book where both working within and across services has made a real difference to outcomes for children and families. Where there is insufficient joining up of the disparate parts within a service, this may, in part, be due to the constant reorganisations that seem to be a feature of all three services. While some of these will turn out to be changes for the better, others turn out to be less successful. While the current round of structural changes to the education, health, and social care systems will take some time to be completed and to embed, the hope is that these will be changes for the better. Integrated care services, the recommendation in *The Independent review of children's social care*, and the proposals in the SEND Green Paper all include ways of bringing the services closer together, which should lead to better outcomes for children and their families, as well as closer ways of working.

What intra- and interagency working can lead to is making sure the child and the family are at the centre, rather than trying to fit them into an existing structure or system. In this way, the support they need can be co-ordinated and everyone can be made aware of the part they are playing and what the other services are providing. Where practicable, having one key worker acting for all the services enables families to cope better with having to deal with different professionals.

As well as focusing on the preceding three developments, this book has mentioned a variety of other partnerships which illustrate the benefits of working together across other services, organisations, and charities. More of this is happening and is to be welcomed. The one area where this may cause difficulties is the Department for Education's (DfE's) interpretation of schools working in partnership, meaning they must be in multi-academy trusts (MATs) rather than recognising that this is one of many types of partnerships schools already have. In December 2022, the Schools Bill was withdrawn. However, as it had much to say about MATs, this may create a pause for thought and an opportunity to press for the recognition of the value of many kinds of partnerships, including but not exclusively in MATs.

Throughout the book, it has been mentioned that there are some encouraging signs of a move towards collaboration and away from competition, both in the health and education services. While there is some way to go, some promising green shoots are there and need to be encouraged as a much more productive way forward.

Co-location

1. Parts of the same service operating in different places when this could be avoided.
2. Different services not being placed together when this is possible.
3. Geographical boundaries getting in the way of what needs to happen.

Following on from the previous section, and looking at parts of the same service being co-located, there have been some encouraging moves to co-locate health clinics for children, making it easier for parents whose children need to be seen by different health professionals. There are schools where mainstream and special schools are co-located and can draw on each other's expertise. Moving beyond this to where there are examples of different services being co-located, there are examples of social workers being based in schools; family hubs being on the site of a school; and the LA's specialist support services being co-located with schools. The benefits of this are enormous, in terms of getting to understand the different cultures that exist and how the different systems operate. It creates opportunities for both formal and informal meetings and for training across the services. But there is so much more that could be done by seizing opportunities when they arise, in terms of both the separate elements of a service working more closely together and in terms of professionals from across the services developing closer professional relationships. In practical terms, it could, for example, result in educational psychologists and therapists being able to spend more time with children and less on travelling. Even if this happens, making sure that professionals, including SENCOs, spend less time on paperwork and more time with pupils is essential if children's outcomes are to improve.

As regards the third point, there is a particular issue about geographical boundaries dictating where a child goes to school. There are many cases where the nearest school to a child is across a county border. Where this involves sizeable groups of children, such as mainstream secondary schools, LAs may work together to make this possible. Where individual children, or perhaps a small group of them, need to go to a special school, parents may have to be really insistent and persistent to get their child into the nearest appropriate school, because it is in a different county. If they do not succeed, time and money is spent by parents or the taxis some SEND pupils require, having to drive further and making the school day longer for these pupils. Having to go further than is necessary also makes it harder for the school and the family to be part of the school community and the one where they live. The situation can be exacerbated by LAs and health having different boundaries. This is difficult to alter, but what could be changed is working more flexibly and thinking of the needs of the child and the family rather than the structures that get in the way of improvements.

Some final thoughts

Whereas it has been possible in this chapter to suggest steps that might be taken to bring about improvements in the way services operate, largely within planned or existing structures, there are issues around the way the education system works that makes it hard for practitioners to influence politicians. This leads to money not always being spent appropriately.

Funding

There are, of course, major concerns about funding across all three services, as well as more generally. However, what is being highlighted here is how to make better use of the money that is available. Spending on education, as on the other services, has increased considerably, but failed to keep pace with demand. The latest plans for improving the SEND and AP system, as well as improving children's social care, are unlikely to receive the amount of funding that is required. If the Schools Bill had gone ahead, with all schools becoming academies and a reduced role for LAs, this would have been yet another example of money being spent on changing structures and systems rather than improving the lives and outcomes for those working and learning within them. When the national curriculum came in, vast sums of money were spent on putting it in place and then a series of steps had to be taken to slim it down, because it was so overloaded it did not fit into the school day. The testing procedures that came along in its wake have resulted in children being tested almost every year they are in primary school. Apart from the adverse effect of this on some pupils, the cost of designing, producing, distributing, and marking new papers every year is enormous. Then Ofsted came in, and although the vast majority of schools are found to be good or outstanding, all schools are inspected regularly. Inspections and inspectors cost a lot of money as well as causing unnecessary workload and stress. These are just a very few examples of how money may not be spent on what matters the most: the pupils and their learning and wellbeing. And it happens because those who work in the profession are not those who make the decisions.

Changing how the education system works

It would be unrealistic to suggest that politicians should stand aside from education, but it should be possible for politicians to take their lead from those who work in education and understand how children learn. The NHS has a Ten-Year Plan. Education is unable to have any plan like this, because no secretary of state for education knows how long he or she will be there and so is keen to make an impact in the shorter term.

In the first chapter of this book, the Levelling Up agenda was discussed. It may indeed be possible to level up parts of the country that feel left behind, but young people cannot be levelled up in the same way. Children learn in different ways; have different interests, abilities, and aptitudes; and are moulded by different life experiences. This is what makes every single child and young person – and indeed every one of us – a unique individual. The more professionals from across the services, the young people themselves, and their families are able to be fully involved in designing and developing the services that are needed, the more likely it is that the experiences and outcomes for children, young people, parents, carers, and wider family members will be on an upward trajectory. Add to this the possibility of education, health, and social care working ever more closely together and the future looks bright.

References

Gov.UK (2014a) *Care Act: Care and Support Statutory Guidance.* Available from https://www.gov.uk/government/publications/care-act-statutory-guidance/care-and-support-statutory-guidance

Gov.UK (2014b) *Children and Families Act.* Available from https://www.legislation.gov.uk/ukpga/2014/6/contents/enacted

Gov.UK (2017) *These Are Our Children. A Review by Dame Christine Lenehan.* Available from https://assets.publishing.service.gov.uk/government/uploads/system/uploads/attachment_data/file/585376/Lenehan_Review_Report.pdf

Gov.UK (2022a) *Health and Care Act.* Available from https://www.legislation.gov.uk/ukpga/2022/31/contents/enacted

Gov.UK (2022b) Schools Bill. Available from https://bills.parliament.uk/bills/3156

Gov.UK (2022c) *SEND Review: Right Support, Right Place, Right Time.* Available from https://www.gov.uk/government/consultations/send-review-right-support-right-place-right-time

MacAlister, J. (2022) *Independent Review of Children's Social Care.* Available from https://childrenssocialcare.independent-review.uk/final-report/

NHS (2014) *Five Year Forward View.* Available from https://www.england.nhs.uk/wp-content/uploads/2014/10/5yfv-web.pdf

Appendix 1

Key documents across education, health and social care 1970–2022

Year	Document	Description
1970	Education Act	All children brought into education
1978	The Warnock Report	"SEN" replaced "handicapped"
1981	Education Act	"Statements" replaced by EHC plans
1988	The Education Reform Act (ERA)	LMS and National Curriculum
1989	Children Act	Developing LA services for children
1993	Education Act	SEN/D Codes of Practice and SENCOs
1995	Disability Discrimination Act (DDA)	
2001	SEN and Disability Act (SENDA)	"Reasonable adjustments"
2003	Report of Laming Inquiry	Led to ECM
2003	Every Child Matters (ECM)	Green Paper
2004	Children Act	Based on ECM
2007	Care Matters: Time for Change	White Paper
2008	Children and Young Persons Act	Reforming the care system
2010	Academies Act	
	Equality Act	Replaced a number of other Acts
2014	Children and Families Act	Brought in SEND Reforms
	Care Act	Greater personalisation of care
	NHS's Five Year Forward Plan	
2017	Children and Social Work Act	Provision for looked after children
	NHS's Five Year Forward Plan: Next Steps	
	Transforming Children and Young People's Mental Health Provision	
		Green Paper
2018	Working Together to Safeguard Children	

2019	NHS'S Long-term Plan	
	Help, Protection, Education: Concluding Children in Need Review	
2021	Skills for Jobs: Lifelong Learning for Opportunity and Growth	
		White Paper
2022	Implementation Programme: Transforming Children and Young People's Mental Health Provision	
February 2022	Levelling Up the United Kingdom	White Paper
March 2022	Opportunity for All: Strong Schools with Great Teachers for Your Child	
		White Paper
March 2022	SEND Review: Right Support, Right Place, Right Time	
		Green Paper
April 2022	Skills and Post-16 Act	
May 2022	Levelling-Up and Regeneration Bill	
	Health and Care Act	Integrated Care Systems (ICSs)
May 2022	Schools Bill	
May 2022	Independent Review of Children's Social Care	
September 2022	Keeping Children Safe in Education (KCSiE)	
		Statutory guidance for schools and colleges

Appendix 2

Recommendations: The independent review of children's social care

Chapter 2

1. A new umbrella of "Family Help" should combine work currently done at targeted early help and section 17, ending handovers and bringing the flexible, non-stigmatising approach at early help to a wider group of families.
2. Eligibility for Family Help should be set out in a sufficient level of detail nationally to give a more consistent understanding of who should receive Family Help, whilst giving enough flexibility to enable professional judgement and empower local Family Help Teams to respond to families' needs.
3. Local Family Help services should be designed in a way that enables families and practitioners to have a conversation about their concerns rather than relying on mechanical referrals. If families are not eligible for Family Help, support should be available in universal and community services and the front door to Family Help should be equipped to link families to this support.
4. Family Help should be delivered by multidisciplinary teams, embedded in neighbourhoods, harness the power of community assets, and tailored to local needs.
5. Government should make an upfront investment of £2 billion in supporting local authorities and their partners to implement the proposed transformation in Family Help. National government pots of funding should be mainstreamed into this funding stream and partners should be incentivised to contribute. Once transformation is complete, the government should ring-fence funding for Family Help to ensure rebalanced investment is sustained.
6. As part of the National Children's Social Care Framework, the government should define outcomes, objectives, indicators of success, and the most effective models for delivering help. Funding should be conditional on meeting the goals of the Framework.
7. Alongside recommendations to strengthen multi-agency partnerships and the role of the Director of Children's Services, the government should consider legislation to put the existence of multidisciplinary Family Help Teams on a statutory footing.
8. Ofsted inspections should reinforce a focus on families receiving high quality, evidence-based help that enables children to thrive and stay safely at home.

9. Government should ensure alignment in how the proposals in the SEND and AP Green Paper and this review are implemented. Government should ask the Law Commission to review the current patchwork of legislation that exists to support disabled children and their families.

Chapter 3

1. All cases of significant harm should be co-worked by an Expert Child Protection Practitioner (in the future this would be someone who had completed our proposed Early Career Framework).
2. Working Together should set expectations on multi-agency capabilities for child protection and the National Children's Social Care Framework should set out effective practice models for joint working.
3. Investment in Family Help will provide resources for multidisciplinary responses to extra familial harms.
4. Government should amend Working Together to introduce a Child Community Safety Plan to clarify where primary harm is not attributable to families, supported by practice guides and the Early Career Framework.
5. There should be clear expectations about partnership responses to extra familial harms across an area and this should be a priority area for learning.
6. Government should integrate funding aimed at preventing individual harms into a single local response to extra familial harms, including enabling areas to integrate their Violence Reduction Unit funding and infrastructure into their local response to extra familial harms.
7. Subject to a positive evaluation of the pilot to devolve responsibility for the National Referral Mechanism decisions for child victims to local areas, government should roll this out to all areas.
8. Government should implement the recommendations of the Taylor review (2016) to simplify the experiences of children in the youth justice system, and as a first step should roll out the flexibility to all local authorities to integrate AssetPlus assessments with child-in-need assessments.
9. Guidance and legislation on information sharing should be strengthened and local safeguarding partners should confirm they have information sharing agreements in place and have audited practice in this area.
10. Government should set a target to achieve frictionless sharing of information between local authority and partner systems by 2027. To enable this they must take an imminent decision on whether to adopt the NHS number as a consistent identifier alongside work by the National Data and Technology Taskforce discussed in Chapter 8.
11. The National Children's Social Care Framework practice guides should promote effective practice for engaging families. Parental representation and support should be offered to all families in child protection.
12. Improve the quality and consistency of local and judicial decision-making through improving the quality and transparency of data and facilitating learning at a local level.

13. The Public Law Working Group should lead work to bring learning from Family Drug and Alcohol Courts and other problem-solving approaches into public law proceedings, to make proceedings less adversarial and improve parents' engagement in the process.

Chapter 4

1. Government should introduce legislation which makes the use of family group decision-making mandatory before a family reaches Public Law Outline. The features and delivery practice of effective family group decision-making should also be included in the National Children's Social Care Framework.
2. A Family Network Plan should be introduced and enabled in law to support and give oversight to family-led alternatives to care.
3. All local authorities should make a financial allowance paid at the same rate as their fostering allowance available for Special Guardians and kinship carers with a Child Arrangement Order (CAO) looking after children who would otherwise be in care.
4. Legal aid should be provided in a range of circumstances where special guardians and kinship carers with a C AO
5. All new special guardians and kinship carers with a CAO should be given kinship leave, which matches the entitlement given to adopters.
6. As part of our recommendation to establish a National Children's Social Care Framework in Chapter 8, local authorities should develop peer support and training for all kinship carers.
7. Government should develop a new legal definition of kinship care, taking a broad range of circumstances into account.
8. Contact arrangements between birth parents, adopted children, and adoptive parents should be assumed by default and modernised through the swift roll out of technology-enabled methods of contact, such as Letterswap.

Chapter 5

1. New and ambitious care standards applicable across all homes for children should be introduced.
2. Regional Care Co-operatives (RCCs) should be established to plan, run, and commission residential care, fostering, and secure care.
3. A windfall tax on profits made by the largest private children's homes providers and independent fostering agencies should be levied to contribute to the costs of transforming the care system.
4. Linked to our recommendations in Chapter 7, Ofsted should be given new powers to oversee and intervene in the children's social care market.
5. The Department for Education should launch a high-profile national foster carer recruitment programme to recruit 9,000 additional foster carers.
6. Local Authorities, and eventually Regional Care Cooperatives, should use family group decision-making to identify important adults that are already known to a child and may be willing to foster.

7. Foster carers should be given delegated authority by default, to take decisions which affect the day-to-day lives of children in their care.
8. All foster carers should be able to access high-quality training and peer support. As part of the National Children's Social Care Framework, all local authorities should develop a model of foster carer support based on the principles of Mockingbird.
9. Independent, opt-out, high-quality advocacy for children in care and in proceedings should replace the existing Independent Reviewing Officer and Regulation 44 Visitor roles. The Children's Commissioner for England should oversee these advocacy services, with the powers to refer children's complaints and concerns to the court.

Chapter 6

1. New legislation should be passed which broadens corporate parenting responsibilities across a wider set of public bodies and organisations.
2. Government should make care experience a protected characteristic, following consultation with care-experienced people and the devolved administrations.
3. National government should issue statutory guidance to local authorities setting out the priority that should be afforded to care-experienced adults in accessing local services such as social housing.
4. Local authorities should redesign their existing Independent Visitor scheme for children in care and care leavers to allow for long-term relationships to be built.
5. As part of the National Children's Social Care Framework, all local authorities should have skilled family-finding support equivalent to or exceeding the work of Lifelong Links in place by 2024 at the very latest.
6. A new lifelong guardianship order should be created, allowing a care experienced person and an adult who loves them to form a lifelong legal bond.
7. As part of our recommendation about Ofsted inspection (Chapter 8), Virtual School Heads should be held accountable for the education attainment of children in care and care leavers up to the age of 25 through Ofsted's ILACS framework. Pupils premium funding should be focused on evidence-led tutoring and mentoring programmes.
8. Virtual School Heads should work to identify more children in care who might benefit from a place at a state or independent day or boarding school, and the Department of Education should create a new wave of state boarding capacity led by the best existing schools.
9. Introduce a new Kitemark scheme for higher education to drive improvements in admissions, access, and support for those with care experience.
10. The Care Leaver Covenant should be refreshed to align with the five missions set out in this report and co-produced with care-experienced people. Employers should be able to apply for a new government-led accreditation scheme which recognises their commitment to supporting care leavers into well-paid jobs.

11. An annual care leaver bursary should be made available to all apprentices up to the age of 25, and employers should be allowed to use unspent apprenticeship levy funds to tailor support for those with care experience.

12. There should be a range of housing options open to young people transitioning out of care or who need to return, such as Staying Put, Staying Close, and supported lodgings. Staying Put and Staying Close should be a legal entitlement and extended to age 23 with an 'opt out' rather than an 'opt in' expectation.

13. Introduce a stronger safety net against care leaver homelessness by removing the local area connection test, ending intentionally homelessness practice, providing a rent guarantor scheme, and increasing the leaving care grant to £2,438 for care-experienced people.

14. The identification and response to poor mental health issues should be a core part of training programmes for any professionals working with children and young people that have involvement with children's services.

15. All local authorities must improve care leaver mental and physical health support, and the National Children's Social Care Framework should promote the most effective multidisciplinary models of doing this.

16. Integrated Care Boards should publish their plans for improving the mental and physical health of those in care and leaving care and routinely publish progress. As part of these plans and a new corporate parenting duty, the Department of Health and Social Care and the NHS should exempt care leavers from prescription charges up to age 25.

17. As part of recommendation in Chapter 8 (improving data collection), the Office for National Statistics should collect and report data on the mortality rate of care leavers and care leaver health outcomes. Government should also launch a new cohort study which tracks the health outcomes of care-experienced people and helps to gather other missing data on housing, education, and employment outcomes.

Chapter 7

1. A nationally led programme should get social workers back to practice through: action on technology to reduce time spent case recording; a mechanism for challenging unnecessary workload drivers; requiring all registered social workers to spend time in practice, and trialling flexible working models around the lives of children and families.

2. Introduce a five-year Early Career Framework for social workers, an Expert Practitioner role, and national pay scales.

3. The government should introduce new national rules on agency usage supported by the development of not-for-profit regional staff banks to reduce costs and increase the stability and quality of relationships children and families receive.

4. To support the development of the wider social care workforce, government should produce a Knowledge and Skills Statement for family support workers; appoint Social Work England to set standards and regulate residential

children's home managers; and fund a new leadership programme that could train up to 700 new managers in the next five years.

Chapter 8

1. A National Children's Social Care Framework should set the objectives and outcomes for children's social care.
2. The National Children's Social Care Framework should include a balanced scorecard of indicators to support learning and improvement. To support this there should be an overhaul of both what data is collected and how those collections work, so that we have more meaningful metrics and more regular data to help drive transparency and learning in the system.
3. The National Children's Social Care Framework should include practice guides, setting out the best evidenced approaches to achieving the objectives set out in the Framework.
4. Data and feedback should be used to prompt local and national learning to continually improve services. At a national level the National Practice Group and National Reform Board should oversee learning from feedback. The evidence and learning landscape should be strengthened through the integration of overlapping What Works Centres, starting with the integration of the Early Intervention Foundation and What Works for Children's Social Care.
5. The National Reform Board should establish a mechanism for local authorities to raise where they feel there are national regulatory blockers to taking a course of action that is in the best interests of children and families, with action taken to address this.
6. The responsibility of multi-agency safeguarding arrangements should be amended to emphasise their role as a strategic forum focused on safeguarding and promoting the welfare of children, with attendance reflecting this.
7. Working Together should be amended to set out clear joint and equal operational responsibilities for partners. The Director of Children's Services should be the primary interface between strategic and operational leaders to facilitate effective multi-agency working.
8. The role of the Director of Children's Services should be reviewed to give clarity to the role following this review, the SEND and AP Green Paper and the Schools White Paper, to reflect their role as a champion for children and families within their area.
9. The individual contribution of partners to achieving the review's vision should be set out clearly in Working Together and reflected in each organisation's strategic plans.
10. Partnerships should become more transparent, including publishing minutes of partnership meetings and the financial contributions of each partner. The Safeguarding Children Reform Implementation Board should be reviewed and strengthened to take a greater leadership role in safeguarding arrangements, including requesting and publishing critical information about partnerships.
11. The Child Safeguarding Practice Review Panel and relevant What Works Centres should take a more hands-on role in promoting evidence and supporting partnerships to improve.

12. Each agency inspectorate should review their framework to ensure there is sufficient focus on individual agency contribution to joint working. Where there are concerns about the functioning of partnerships, then joint inspections, with a judgement attached, should be triggered.

13. Schools should be made a statutory safeguarding partner and contribute to the strategic and operational delivery of multi-agency working.

14. Government should incentivise greater partner contributions through requiring partners to publish their financial contribution and making receiving the full funding for reform contingent on partner contributions.

15. National government should ensure it has an oversight mechanism in place to ensure policy relating to children and families is aligned in contact with children's social care. Government programmes should be streamlined to support these reforms and youth justice policy should move to the Department for Education.

16. Government should introduce an updated funding formula for children's service, and take greater care to ensure that changes in government policy that impact the cost of delivering children's social scare are accompanied by additional resources for local government.

17. Ofsted inspection should be reformed to increase transparency in how judgements are made, ensure inspection applies a rounded understanding of being 'child focused' and to ensure inspection supports the proposed reforms.

18. Strengthen intervention powers and introduce Regional Improvement Commissioners to provide more robust challenge in the system. Ensure there is a clear expert improvement offer for local authorities.

19. Government should establish a National Data and Technology Taskforce to drive progress on implementing the review's three priority recommendations to: achieve frictionless data sharing by 2027, drastically reduce the time social workers spend on case recording, and improve the use and collection of data locally.

20. The Department for Education should have a proactive strategy on making better use of data in children's social care, including a strategy for data linking for children's social care with other data sources that makes use of the ONS-integrated data service.

Index

Page numbers in **bold** indicate tables.